Praise for "Scott Sedita's Guide T

"Coming from North Dakota there was̶n̶ ̶t̶ ̶a̶ ̶l̶o̶t̶ ̶o̶f̶ ̶t̶h̶e̶ world of entertainment, so I was understandably apprehensive and intimidated by the spectacle that is Los Angeles. I was curious about acting -- however I was seriously lacking in the confidence department. I am so thankful for Scott giving me the initial push that got the ball rolling for me. Though it will always be a work in progress, I can attribute my beginnings to Mr. Scott Sedita."

-Josh Duhamel, Actor (*Las Vegas, Transformers*)

"I believe the main reason I continue to work is because I strive to be confident and real. I would have had no chance of achieving either of those if it wasn't for Scott Sedita. His ability to prepare the actor for both the craft of acting and the accompanying business is unparalleled in my experience."

-Geoff Stults, Actor (*October Road*)

"Not only is Scott Sedita incredibly skilled at coaching, but his advice and words of wisdom have been indispensable to me. And now he shares it with all of you."

-Jennifer Finnigan, Actor (*Close to Home*)

"Scott Sedita's Guide To Making It In Hollywood...will inspire and empower you to become a successful actor. Get ready for some changes with this book!"

-Jay Kenneth Johnson, Actor (*Days of Our Lives*)

"Sedita has a fresh, unique approach to 'making it' as an actor. This is a book for actors that want to be in it for the long haul and are focused on achieving success."

-Mark Teschner, Emmy Award-Winning Casting Director

"This book is like having a personal life coach guiding you through your acting career. It should be required reading for anyone who wants to make it in this business. A MUST READ!!!"

-Terry Berland, Casting Director

"Scott has done it again! The information in this book is aimed at actors at all levels. I learned for myself and received so much to pass on to my students. 'Scott Sedita's Guide To Making It In Hollywood' answers: how do I improve, how do I better my chances, how can I enhance my career and my life? I urge you to read this book...NOW!"

-Judy Kerr, Author of "Acting Is Everything"

"I always recommend Scott's books and classes to actors who have talent but need no-nonsense, practicable direction to make the most of it. No guru, no flatterer, no flim-flam name-dropper, Scott combines a shrewd business sense with absolute truth-telling."

-David Rambo, Writer/Producer (*CSI*)

"Scott Sedita's Guide To Making It In Hollywood is a must read for anyone thinking about entering the very challenging business of acting. Scott knows the business from many angles -- as an agent, casting director and acting coach. This book is full of invaluable advice and insight into the world of acting."

-Susan Vash, Casting Director

"Imagine you have a really good friend who knows EVERYTHING about breaking into the acting game and you'll have some idea what's it's like to read this engaging and informative book."

-Jed Seidel, Executive Producer

"Scott Sedita is an inspiration in person and on the page. His new book is a recipe for success for anyone who really wants it!"

-Mary Lou Belli, Emmy Award-Winning Director

"Scott's book is so smart, so complete, so full of real, practical advice that I'm actually tempted to step from behind the camera to in front of the camera!"
-Rob Lotterstein, TV Executive Producer

"Scott Sedita's simple and practical concepts will assist the actor to have both the confidence and the tools to start on that very difficult path to becoming a working actor in Hollywood."
-Victoria Morris, Talent Agent, Kazarian/Spencer & Associates

"Scott's enthusiasm for his work and his extraordinary insight in human nature makes this book a 'must-have' for any aspiring actor."
-Ellen Pittleman, Film Executive, Paramount Pictures

"This book has something new to say. The clarity and wisdom is immediately understandable and personally useful. A 'must read' book for every actor."
-Steven Nash, Talent Manager, Arts and Letters Management

"I wanted to get better at comedy, so I went to Scott Sedita. A few months later, I booked a series regular on a sitcom! Karma? Maybe. Sedita? Absolutely!"
-Jonathan Chase, Actor (*Knight Rider*)

"Scott Sedita highlights the real obstacles that face the professional actor, and gives the advice and counsel so desperately needed in this 'overnight-sensation' town. He demystifies and debunks years of silly thinking that has plagued millions of actors as they embark on a career in acting."
-Peter Kluge, Talent Manager, Impact Artists Group

Scott Sedita's

Guide To
Making It In
Hollywood

3 Steps to Success

3 Steps to Failure

Atides Publishing, Los Angeles, California

Scott Sedita's Guide To Making It In Hollywood
3 Steps to Success
3 Steps to Failure

Published by:
Atides Publishing
526 N. Larchmont Blvd.
Los Angeles, CA 90004, USA
AtidesPub@aol.com

ISBN: 978-0-9770641-1-3
Library of Congress Control Number: 2008923937

Cover photo: Collin Stark
Cover and interior design: Andrew Deutsch
Editor: Jim Martyka

First printing: 2008
Printed in the United States of America

To my father, Charles…

…who has always believed in me.

TABLE OF CONTENTS

Acknowledgments

I would like to thank…

…editor Jim Martyka for helping me organize my thoughts, ideas, notes and philosophies into a book.

…my good friend Frank Salamone for sharing his experience, advice and opinions.

…my mentor Judy Kerr for her continued support, guidance and help throughout this process.

…all the "readers" who helped me edit this book; Deborah Quayle, Rob Lotterstein, Kelly Valentine, Patrick Munoz, Todd Rohrbacher, Tony Rago, Claes Lilja and Terri Cole-Juhasz.

…my loving family for always being there and supporting me throughout my many careers: my father Chuck, Helen, Peter, Guy, Samantha, Van, my Uncle Pat and Aunt Jo, my cousin Rosetta and her husband Charlie, my cousin Don and my dear Aunt Lois.

…my mother Doris who is and always will be my guardian angel.

…my friends for all their encouragement, love and humor; my ever-supportive partner Nicholas Proietti, Ed Fitz, Ellen Pittleman, Phil Oster, Tony Wisniewski and everyone else I might be forgetting. Sorry once again.

…the teachers at Scott Sedita Acting Studios for helping to make our studio the success that it is today.

…all those actors that bravely and courageously shared their experiences and stories with me for this book.

…all of my students who inspire me and challenge me to become a better teacher and a more creative human being. You all make me proud and help me remember why I'm doing this in the first place.

We are all born with innate abilities, skills and talents. What we choose to do with these gifts defines who we are and who we can become. After we acknowledge these gifts, we can choose to embrace them, pursue them and turn them into a career. And if we choose to do so, then we all need a plan, a roadmap to help us fulfill our dreams, our destiny, our life's work.

This book is a guide for all those people born with the ability to act and the desire and drive to turn that gift into a career. This book is your guide to becoming a successful actor.

Your journey begins...now.

AUTHOR'S PREFACE

I was born with the innate ability to act, write and direct...and that's pretty much what I did throughout my childhood.

I was always performing, putting on mini-extravaganzas in the living room or backyard of my house in Glen Cove, New York. I appeared in every school play. While I considered myself a leading man, I was often put into a supporting role (or worse...the chorus)! In retrospect, I guess it wasn't likely that a funny, chubby, curly-haired kid with a Long Island accent would play Tom Sawyer or Prince Charming. Nevertheless, I knew I wanted to be an actor.

Over time, that funny, chubby, curly-haired kid grew into a tall, fit and trim teenager. Gone were the supporting roles! I now played the lead in all the school plays and community theatre shows. I also wrote, produced and directed elaborate productions in the high school auditorium and community centers.

When it was time for college, I was accepted into the acting program at Boston University's School of Fine Arts. I immediately noticed the varying degrees of talent among my fellow students: some actors were brimming with talent while others had a harder time accessing it. I also noticed the different degrees of confidence each actor possessed: some came to the program with a solid foundation of confidence already instilled in them, while others seemed unsure, hesitant and lacking faith. There was also a clear distinction between the actors who had more drive, passion and perseverance about the prospects of an acting career than those who didn't.

It was during my second year of acting school that I realized I no longer wanted to act. I discovered that I didn't have a great "want" to become a professional actor, and it became apparent that if I didn't truly want it, it wasn't going to happen. At the same time, I found myself more interested in writing and directing scenes for actors. So, I chose to leave the acting program to pursue those other creative avenues.

I didn't go far. Actually, I went right across the street to B.U.'s Film School. For the next two years, I worked diligently at making as many student films and TV projects as possible. I enlisted my acting school friends from across the street to appear in my productions. I also worked hard to make industry contacts in Los Angeles…and it paid off!

By the time I graduated, I had a job waiting for me in Hollywood. But the day *after* I graduated, I got a phone call informing me that there was a writers' strike and the job was no longer available. With no other options, I moved back home to New York City.

Needing work, I took a job as an agent's assistant with a well-known talent agency called Writers and Artists. I quickly became very adept at my job. I had an instinctual understanding of the workings of being an agent -- talking to casting directors, spotting new talent, taking care of actors.

I worked for Writers and Artists for a year until I accepted a position as a full-fledged agent at the Mary Ellen White Agency. I was 22 years old and the youngest franchised agent in New York City. Every night, I went out to showcases and discovered new actors. I signed them, guided them, nurtured them and groomed them for success. And it worked! Or should I say, *they* worked. After a two-year stint at the Mary Ellen White Agency, I moved to a hot new agency called Frontier Booking International (FBI).

During my time at FBI, I was instrumental in discovering and building the careers of several of today's top stars, including Courteney Cox, Matt Le Blanc, Dylan Walsh, Teri Polo, Vincent D'Onofrio and Christopher Meloni. As an agent, I worked very closely with my clients. I guided them on building their careers as well as their craft. Considering my acting training, I often coached my actors before they went out on their auditions. I enjoyed the process of working with actors and seeing them grow as artists.

Being an agent was exciting but there was something nagging at me. I still had the need to explore my creativity; I wanted to write. I started taking TV and film script writing classes after work. Then, one day I had an epiphany. I was sitting at my desk and suddenly thought, "Does being an agent still make me happy?" The answer was "No."

After nearly a decade of representing actors, I decided to call it quits. At the top of my game, I chose to give up being a talent agent and I moved to Los Angeles to pursue a writing career.

I had a great beginning. I got an agent, took meetings with network and studio execs and booked some TV writing gigs. Then the momentum started to wane...and so did my desire. I was waiting for my big break: to get on a TV show as a staff writer and it wasn't happening quickly enough.

I was also now in my mid-30s and I wanted a life of stability and security. Luckily I had a great "survival job" that would soon present a brand new career opportunity.

As I was pursuing my writing career, I worked with casting director Danny Goldman, where I got a unique perspective on the casting process. As I watched thousands of actors audition, I very quickly recognized the experienced actor versus the inexperienced actor, the talented versus the not-so-talented. I saw, once again, how an actor's confidence plays a major role in achieving success. I also got a view of how actors -- through various forms of fear -- sabotaged themselves in an audition.

I witnessed how important it was for actors to understand who they were and what type(s) they played best. The actors who knew themselves were the ones that consistently worked. I got excited when an actor was right for a role, worked hard, and booked it.

During my time casting, I ran into an actress I used to represent. She asked me to coach her for a TV series audition. I did and she booked the job. This lead me to start offering acting classes (at Danny Goldman's) as well as private coaching sessions, which helped many actors to book jobs on films, TV shows and soaps.

I quickly discovered that I loved coaching actors. There was a thrill in seeing an actor seek, find and speak the truth. Actors responded well to my style of coaching, my acting techniques and my straightforward approach to the business. I not only wanted actors to learn the craft of acting, I also wanted them to understand what it takes to have a career in acting.

I found a whole new kind of satisfaction in teaching and coaching that I had never experienced before. I was now at another crossroads and I was taking stock in what I wanted to do with my life. The choice became clear...I wanted to redirect all my creative energy into a career as an Acting Coach.

One evening after work, I drove to Larchmont, a quaint, hip section of Hollywood, to meet a friend for coffee. On the way, I spotted a "Space for Rent" sign on a building on Larchmont Blvd. I thought if I ever opened an acting studio, this would be a great location: upscale, quiet, safe. So I stopped and checked out the space. It was perfect! I decided right then and there, this was going to be my acting studio. I signed a three-year lease.

I opened my studio in 1998 with high hopes and only 10 students -- which didn't even cover my rent. During the day, I ran the business and coached actors. At night and on weekends, I taught acting to kids, teens, young adults and adults. I worked hard to build up my courses, my student enrollment, my studio and my presence in the industry.

Now, 10 years later, Scott Sedita Acting Studios has over 200 students, a staff of six acting coaches and a reputation as one of the leading acting studios in Hollywood. Many young talented actors have gone from my studio to become successful actors on film and TV, including Josh Duhamel, Brandon Routh and Jennifer Finnigan. I continue to see many more potential stars walk through my studio doors every day. That, to me, is more exciting and satisfying than anything I've done in the past.

At this point in my life, all my talent, confidence and perseverance has paid off. I'm a successful acting coach, I've authored two books, I give seminars all over the country, I consult for networks, I work on television and best of all, I get to work with actors on a continual basis.

I feel very fortunate that I've been able to explore several avenues of this business, and that I've been able to experience

what it feels like to act, direct, agent, write, cast and most of all...
coach.

We are all faced with opportunities, obstacles and choices
when it comes to our careers.

As you begin your journey as an actor in Hollywood, *you*
will also be faced with opportunities, obstacles and most of all,
choices. They will all lead you somewhere in your career and they
will all help you grow as individual artists. Who we are and who
we become are dictated by the choices we make in our life and in
our career.

It's those choices -- and the conflicts, successes, failures, joys,
pain and possibility that accompany them -- that form our lives
and will eventually tell our stories.

Embrace this choice to pursue your acting dream, celebrate
your decision to be an actor and enjoy the experience that this
acting career will bring to your life. Most of all, love what you
do.

Scott Sedita
2008

INTRODUCTION

Recently, at the Larchmont Deli, a few blocks from my acting studio, I ran into a former student of mine who I hadn't seen in a few years. I'll call him...Brent.

As Scott stands at the counter ordering an over-stuffed gyro, Brent, a young, good-looking actor approaches.

BRENT: (*CHEERFULLY*) Hey, Scott.

SCOTT: Hey, Brent! (*THEY HUG IT OUT*)

BRENT: Good to see you!

SCOTT: Good to see you, too!

At this point in the conversation, I would usually ask an actor I hadn't seen in a while how their career was going. But something inside -- an instinct perhaps -- led me to rephrase the question...

SCOTT: So, how's...*life* treating you?

BRENT: Good. Yeah, life is good, very good.

SCOTT: Good to hear!

BRENT: Except I've been depressed ever since I gave up acting.

SCOTT: Oh, well, that's certainly not good to hear. I mean...the depressed part.

BRENT: I was there, you know? I was on my way...and then I just let it all slip through my fingers.

A little history: When Brent first came to my acting studio a few years back, he was a very charismatic young man with an innate ability to act as well as an agent who was grooming him for stardom. All Brent needed to do was study his craft, build his confidence, and stay focused and he'd be on his way. And that's what Brent did...for the first six months.

For the next few months, Brent's commitment to his craft and career started waning. Even though he booked some small acting gigs, he started to "flake" when it came to class. He didn't do his homework, he'd procrastinate, he'd show up late or he'd just miss class altogether. He even began missing auditions! Suddenly, Brent's acting career was full of distractions and he took too many wrong actions, which ultimately put him on a path to self-sabotage.

When I confronted him, he had a million excuses: family obligations, friends in need, roommate problems, girlfriend drama, money issues, etc. You name it...Brent had an excuse for it. As a matter of fact, those excuses and the "drama" surrounding the stories he weaved became his only opportunity to act! Eventually, Brent dropped out of acting class and his agent dropped him. He decided he needed to "take a break from acting."

Nikko, the guy behind the counter, hands Scott his over-stuffed gyro as Brent looks on.

BRENT: So Scott, funny that I'm bumping into you because I thought about you the other day.

SCOTT: How so?

BRENT: Well...(*TAKES A DEEP BREATH*)...I woke up one morning and it was three years later.

SCOTT: (*NODS KNOWINGLY*) Oh, I see.

To some this might sound like an odd non sequitur. But for those who've studied with me, it makes perfect sense. You see, I frequently remind my actors to "be focused," "keep their eye on their goal" and "stay on the path." But for those actors who get distracted and veer off, especially in L.A....well, here's what happens:

BRENT: Yeah, I realize that I let a lot of...stuff get in my way from doing what I really came out here to do, you know? And now...it's three years later.

Unfortunately, this happens all too often for actors, especially those pursuing a career in Hollywood. You wake up one morning, it's *three years later* and you say to yourself, "What the hell have I been doing with my time?"

You realize that you have not met your goals, you have not lived up to your potential, you have not accomplished any of the things that brought you to Hollywood in the first place. You've wasted time, paralyzed by fear and you've self-sabotaged! You've spent more time *talking* about having a career than actually *having a career*!

BRENT: So, I guess I have to start all over, huh?

SCOTT: Yes, Brent, I guess you do. But hey, at least now you know what not to do.

BRENT: (*LAUGHS*) That's for sure. I could write a book!

SCOTT: How about I write the book and you concentrate on your acting career?

This book is not only about how to help you succeed in your acting career; it's also about how to help you avoid failure. It's about not letting those three years pass you by. And if they have passed you by, it's about how to quickly get you back on the path.

This book is a "call to arms" to all those dreamers who want, wish, hope and pray to have a career as an actor in Hollywood.

So stop sitting around and dreaming. Take action! Don't just dream it. Do it! I will be your guide, navigating you on your road to success. I will also show you how to avoid the pitfalls. I will hold your hand on one page and kick your ass on the next. No matter where you are in your career, no matter what has happened in the past, it's all about the present. It's about what you're doing *now.*

I will draw upon my 25 years in the industry as an actor, director, agent, writer, casting director and acting coach to show you what works and what doesn't. I will point out the necessary ingredients to a winning acting career and how you can use them. I will also identify the most common obstacles and tell you how you can avoid sabotaging yourself and your career. Lastly, I will tell you stories of the many successful actors I've worked with and what they did to make it in Hollywood.

The journey to a successful acting career is a long one and it's not easy. There's the thrill of victory as well as the agony of defeat. But if you want it, if you truly want it with your heart, mind, body and soul, you can have it. You can become a successful actor.

SECTION ONE

THE WANT

How do you make it in Hollywood?

Well, before I get to that, let me briefly share a technique I use in my class. I call it...**The Want.**

I like the word *Want*. It's a simple enough word and by "simple," I mean clear and specific. When used as a verb, it means to feel a need or desire for something as in, "I *want* to read this book." It also can be used as a noun as in, "What is my *Want?*"

In my acting class, I always ask my students, "What is your character's Want?" I ask them what they (as the character) want in the scene, in the script, in the moment? Is their Want to change someone's opinion, acquire an object, gain another's affection or complete an urgent task? What is driving their character in the scene?

Many acting coaches use the word *Objective* to specify the character's need, as in "What is your character's *Objective?*" For me, the word Objective is too cerebral, too heady. We rarely use that word in our everyday life. I mean, when confronting your boss for more money, you don't say, "My *Objective* is to get a raise." You say, "I *Want* a raise...now!"

The word Want is primal, visceral and raw. We use it every day to express our most basic and most passionate needs, urges and desires: I want to eat. I want to sleep. I want you to listen to me. I want to make love. I want to leave. I want *you* to leave. I want to read this book in peace!

Next time you approach a scene, first define your character's Want and then say it out loud. For example, *"I want you to listen to me."* Repeat this sentence as many times as possible with several different intentions (to plead, to shame, to seduce, to crush, etc.) and see what organically happens inside your body before, during and after the exercise.

You will instantly come alive! You will feel energized, you will feel a tingling, you will feel strong about your intentions, your choices. You will feel empowered because you know what you want. Repeatedly stating your Want is an effective technique to use before entering any scene. I call it "revving your engine."

DISCOVERING YOUR WANT

Discovering the Want of your character and achieving that Want is a powerful tool in your acting craft. It helps you uncover and tap into your character's true desire. It's the basis for a strong performance.

Likewise, using the Want is equally as empowering when you apply it to your acting *career*. Actors who know what they want in their acting work, and use strong and clever intentions and tactics to get what they want, are more apt to successfully apply that approach to their acting careers.

The truth is, that Want is vital to making it in Hollywood. If you don't really want it, then this is not the path for you. If you don't truly commit to your Want, then you won't have an acting career -- it will be a futile journey. It's best to save your energy and your time and choose a career that will keep you interested, sane and ultimately happy.

It's important to understand that you are entering a highly competitive market where there is no room for those actors who aren't fully committed. Truth be told, those actors who *are* fully committed are waiting for those less committed actors to pack up and leave. It happens every day. It's survival of the fittest, Hollywood style.

So, what do you want in your career?

This is the first of several **Exercises** you will find throughout this book. They are all designed to help you grow in your craft as well as your career. Some of them might seem basic and others might seem more difficult. But in all of these exercises, you must be willing to open your heart, mind and body for them to be effective. As actors, you must always be willing to "go there."

Exercise: I want

First, find a chair and get comfortable. Sit up with both feet on the ground and close your eyes. Say the words "I want" softly to yourself. Without any intention or intonations, let it effortlessly leave your lips. Then, say it again, this time in your full speaking voice and see how it feels.

Now begin to say "I want" with as much passion and feeling as you can muster. Take a deep breath, reach deep inside yourself and feel the words form in your gut, rise through your chest, enter into your mouth and come out through your lips.

I want!

(PASSIONATELY)

I WANT!

(MORE PASSIONATELY!)

I WANT!!

(EVEN MORE PASSIONATELY!!!!)

I WANT!!!!!

If you were fully committed to the exercise, then it felt great! You dug deep, released something strong and powerful, and verbalized some great need and desire. You opened yourself up to the prospect of actually wanting something, voiced it, and put it out to the universe for all to hear.

Just speaking the words "I want" out loud organically sends an active message from your brain to your body. It triggers your survival instinct, which releases a vitality inside of you that prepares you to get what you want against all odds. It pumps you up and heightens your senses. You feel alive, self-assured and grounded. Voicing your Want is as primal as a baby's cry. When infants cry, they're really just saying, "I want to be held, I want to eat, I want to be changed...now!"

As adults, many of us feel we don't have the right to state what we want. We have been conditioned through our upbringing and life's circumstances to refrain from saying what we truly want for fear of rejection, humiliation or abandonment. Therefore, we can become angry, passive-aggressive, whiney or depressed...and not even realize *why*. That all comes down to Fear, which I'll address in Section Two of this book.

As an actor embarking on a career, you must recognize your Fear, experience it, work through it, and overcome it. You must feel that you can not only *state* what you want but also *get* what you want. It's vital to your success. But first, you need to be clear about what it *is* that you want.

So, what DO you want in your acting career? Take your time to think about it. Then write it down below:

I want to...

You may have written *I want to...*"be a film star," "be on a sitcom," "win an Oscar," "be a Working Actor!" These are all perfect Wants and they all share the same desire...to be a successful actor. So for right now, write down:

I want to be a successful actor.

Now that you've written it down (perhaps for the first time), say it out loud:

I want to be a successful actor.

Great! For many of you, this might have been the first time you heard yourself say it out loud. Good for you! You've just specified and identified what it is that you *really want* in your career.

Let's put it out there again so you can truly acknowledge it and embrace it. First, say it softly to *yourself* three times:

`I want to be a successful actor.`

`I want to be a successful actor.`

`I want to be a successful actor.`

Say it out loud in your full speaking voice for the universe to hear.

`I want to be a successful actor.`

Say it three more times, each time louder and more passionate than the last.

`I want to be a successful actor.`

`I want to be a successful actor!`

`I WANT TO BE A SUCCESSFUL ACTOR!`

Congratulations! You've just stated your need, your desire, your Want! You put it out there and the universe has officially heard you…and so have your neighbors.

Let's take it one step further. Let's *visualize* your Want. Visualizing your Want will put both your conscious and subconscious mind to work at manifesting your vision and making it come true.

Once again, get comfortable in your chair, close your eyes and clear your mind. Picture yourself on a film set. You have the lead role. You've just finished a scene, the director yells, "Cut!" and you feel amazing.

The adrenaline of your performance is still pumping through your veins. The crew gives you a round of applause as you take a quick, appreciative bow. The PA brings you a bottle of water and gives you a thumb's up.

The director comes over, gives you a hug, and tells you what a pleasure it is to work with you and what a great talent you are. The extras are looking at you with awe and admiration while your co-stars pat you on the back. The assistant director talks to you about tomorrow's shoot as he walks you back to your trailer.

Once you get inside your trailer, the adrenaline eases away into a feeling of great satisfaction. You have given it your all today. More importantly, you've done what you set out to do, you've become a successful working actor and you feel proud, excited and ready to do it all again.

We have all dreamed about what it would be like to be a successful actor. We have all fantasized about working on a set, being on *The Tonight Show,* or winning an Oscar! Having these fantasies is not only important to realizing a dream, but also empowering and vital to fulfilling that dream.

Knowing, stating and visualizing what you want and working to achieve your Want fearlessly, passionately and consistently will open the door to making it in Hollywood.

Before you walk through that door, though, you need to pledge to always stay *committed* to your craft, your career, your destiny.

ACTOR CONTRACT

I, _____ promise to do all that I can to achieve my Want. I pledge to always work hard, take advantage of any and all opportunities, appreciate the experience, and enjoy the journey. I promise to go after my Want passionately and diligently and to stop at nothing at reaching my dream of becoming a successful actor.

_____

Sign and date

THE THREE STEPS
TO SUCCESS

TALENT
CONFIDENCE
PERSEVERANCE

CHAPTER 1
TALENT

Of the Three Steps to Success, **Talent** is most important.

While the other two steps, Confidence and Perseverance, are vital to making it in Hollywood, neither will help you if you don't first have Talent...more specifically, the Talent to act.

Having Talent means you have an innate ability to do something well and the potential to do something great.

We can all watch a classic movie or TV show and recognize Talent. For the most part, we can all agree on great performances.

We can appreciate the work of Tom Hanks, Meryl Streep, Al Pacino, Julianne Moore, Johnny Depp, Cate Blanchett, Daniel Day-Lewis, as well as the great television actors who appear in shows like *Law & Order, Friends, The Sopranos, Will & Grace, The West Wing, Sex and the City, Grey's Anatomy, Lost, House M.D., Mad Men* and *Brothers & Sisters*.

All of these actors have that instinct, that intrinsic ability to act...and they choose to use that Talent to its fullest. To be a successful actor, you not only need the Talent to act, you also need a great desire to *show it off.*

First, though, you need to discover *your* Talent. In this chapter, I will teach you how to uncover, acknowledge, access and maintain your Talent. That starts with taking a look at where Talent comes from.

WHERE DOES TALENT COME FROM?

Throughout this book, I will frequently discuss how our individual *genes* impact who we are and what we do. Genes are specific sequences of DNA that can be found in each cell in the human body. When we talk about our genetic makeup, we usually think about the physical attributes that were passed down to us from our family tree: "I got mom's freckles, dad's thick hair or grandpa's stocky frame."

As research progresses, scientists are now able to specify that certain types of genes passed down to us from our parents and grandparents may go beyond just physical characteristics and into mannerisms, diseases, moods, personality traits...and even Talent.

I have always believed that actors are predisposed to a specific gene that gives them their unique Talent, their natural ability to pretend, to perform, to act. I call this inherited cluster of DNA...

The Acting Gene

The Acting Gene is where your artistic instincts reside. Having the Acting Gene is a gift. Wherever you think this gift came from -- God, the Universe, your ancestors, your uncle Bob -- you have to first acknowledge that you have a gift. Whether or not you turn it into a career is a whole other story (more on that later).

If you *don't* have the Acting Gene, I'm afraid you'll never be an actor.

At the very least, you'll never be able to sustain a *career* as an actor. I know that might sound harsh, but the reality is...not everyone can act. How could they? I mean, what kind of world would it be if everyone had the Acting Gene?

Also, no matter what you've heard, you cannot rely on your good looks, your winning personality or your "connections" to have a professional acting career. While they may certainly help you get your foot in the door, they're no substitute for having Talent. Talent is not something you can pick up at the mall or purchase online -- it's not for sale.

And just because you've done a stint on a reality show, that doesn't mean you suddenly have the ability to act. Appearing on shows like *Survivor, The Amazing Race, Big Brother, The Bachelor* or *Beauty and the Geek* might give you "15 minutes of fame" or a career as a celebrity, but it doesn't necessarily make you an actor. The Talent to *act* makes you an actor.

You can't get Talent by enrolling in a competition show like *Dancing with the Stars, So You Think You Can Dance* and *Fight For Fame*. Case in point: *American Idol*…if there's an Acting Gene, there must be a Singing Gene, right? Well, the one thing we've most certainly learned from the Audition portion of *American Idol* is that if they can't sing…*they can't sing!* No advice, no support, no scathing criticism from Simon Cowell will ever make them singers. They can practice all they want, but if they don't have an innate ability to sing, they'll never become professional singers -- in this case, practice will *never* make perfect.

Were you born with The Acting Gene?

At its most basic, the craft of acting asks you to pretend. That's really what acting is…pretending. So growing up, were you good at pretending? Could you make others believe you when you were creating an alternative truth?

The best way to measure your Acting Gene is to look to your childhood. Throughout this book, I will ask you to examine your youth to see what innate instincts you came into this world with and how your upbringing influenced them. It's important to look back at who you were before you can analyze and assess who you are now -- both as an actor and as a person. It will give you perspective on where you came from, what you were born with. It lets you know your potential and helps you discover what you still need to do to accomplish your goals.

By looking back on our childhood, we can see how we were naturally and instinctually guided to do something before the fear, obstacles and limitations came into our life.

Let's assume you all have the Acting Gene...however developed it may be.

As a child, rate your Acting Gene on a scale of "1 - 3," with 3 being the most brimming with raw Talent. Try and assess just how much Talent you were born with and displayed as a small child... from the time you were born to about five years old.

If you're having trouble remembering, ask your parents, grandparents, siblings or whoever raised you. Sometimes our own early memories can be blurred or distorted. Family can be a valuable resource for helping you examine your childhood history. Ask them questions about how you were as an infant and child, and then do the scale.

Talent Scales:

The Instinctual Years (birth - five years old)

1 Rating: You didn't pretend as much. You were more practical. Even as a toddler, you took things at face value and really only focused on what was in front of you, whether it was an object, a task, etc. You didn't drift off into a fantasy world. You didn't have an active imaginary life. You didn't wonder.

2 Rating: You had your own imaginary worlds that you could escape to along with imaginary friends. You played dress up, had tea parties, played with Barbies, G.I. Joes, Matchbox Cars. You had a desire to perform, to entertain. You were naturally curious. You could take any object and keep yourself amused with it because you used your imagination. There was awe and wonder in your eyes.

3 Rating: You showed early signs of being a child prodigy. You walked and talked at a very early age. You were a quick learner and took direction very well. You had a vast imaginary life; you loved to pretend. You were the center of attention and enjoyed being that way. You were always "on." You were so bursting with Talent that you may have even worked professionally in commercials, TV and film (think the Olsen twins, Mary Kate and Ashley).

At this early age, it is primarily your instincts that play the major role in determining where you would fall on the scale. Your instincts -- in this case, your Acting Gene -- determine how much Talent you were born with and how much you displayed it. But that can change as you grow, especially during your Formative Years.

There are some people that start off as little performers and then as they grow, they become more shy and reserved. They move away from their Talent and into more practical and intellectual professions. There are others who start out more shy and reserved and suddenly break out of their shell to become performers. Once again, using a rating scale of 1 - 3, assess how much Talent you had growing up in your Formative Years.

The Formative Years (six years old - late teens)

1 Rating: You knew you could pretend and even act, but you never practiced or even really accessed your Acting Gene. You might have appeared in a school play or two, but you really didn't utilize or take advantage of your Talent until adulthood.

2 Rating: You put on shows in your living rooms and garages for your friends, neighbors and family. You enjoyed being the center of attention, perhaps even being the class clown. You developed an interest and appreciation for the Arts. You acted in school plays, community theatre, and may have even become professional, having moderate success in commercials, TV and film. You knew at an early age that you wanted to grow up to be an actor.

3 Rating: The 3's *are* the prodigies in the Acting Gene. They are usually child and teen actors with raw, remarkable ability to pretend at an early age. Think of past child stars like Jodie Foster, Ricky Schroder, Macaulay Culkin, Anna Paquin, Haley Joel Osment, Dakota Fanning and the cast of the *Harry Potter* films. Much like child prodigies in music, science and spelling, these kids translate their raw Talent into startling success. The Talent is pouring out of them so much that they HAVE to act.

Where do you fit on the Formative Years scale and how did that change from the Instinctual Years scale? Did you start out as a 2 on the Instinctual Years scale and drop to a 1 on the Formative Years scale? Did you move up or did you stay the same?

Why does your Talent change? Well, because your Talent instincts are only part of the equation. As you grow up, there are a number of other factors that affect not just your Talent but also how much you decide to use it, none more so than your upbringing.

Talent comes from your upbringing

Your upbringing doesn't have as much of an effect on your ability to act, your Talent, as it does on the other Steps to Success, Confidence and Perseverance. However, it can influence how much you accessed your Talent and to what degree.

Whether you come from a supportive household or had to deal with loss, loneliness or abandonment in your youth, you could discover and develop your Talent just the same. Many great actors have come from dysfunctional backgrounds as opposed to those with a little more stability.

But, as with most skills and talents, there is something to be said about creative encouragement. Having a healthier upbringing with parents or guardians who applauded your ability to act, pushed you to explore it further, and rewarded your successes may have made your Talent development a little easier.

That said, looking back on how you were raised can help you asses how fully developed your Talent is at this point in your life.

Are you ACTOR A or ACTOR B?

ACTOR A: Did you have parents who not only acknowledged your innate ability, but also encouraged you to use it? Did they let you explore your imaginary life? Did they give you the positive reinforcement you needed to bolster your creativity? Did they read to you, give you coloring books or other toys that would help you use your Talent? Did they sign you up for acting, singing or dance classes? Did they come see your plays, recitals and concerts?

Or

ACTOR B: Did your parents, because of their own life circumstances, not spend as much time with you or support you and your creative nature -- physically, emotionally or even financially? Did they fail to give you the tools to explore your imaginary life? Were they unable to inspire and reward you for your creativity? Did they discourage you from participating in activities? Did they look down upon acting as if it wasn't even an option for a career?

If you identified more with ACTOR A, you're probably more familiar with accessing your Acting Gene...or at least you feel comfortable with where you are in your acting ability. You probably spent your childhood exploring the actor in you and you're not emotionally afraid to perform...you're not blocked. You have explored your Talent and you look forward to creative challenges.

If you identified more with ACTOR B, you may have a great deal of Talent, but it might be harder to uncover and break out of its shell. Accessing your Talent may be a bit tougher because you haven't really been taught how. You might even feel emotionally blocked or fearful to act. Although you might be excited to explore your Talent, it's still foreign, unfamiliar, maybe even scary to you. You might have to work harder to break through that fear and tap into your creativity, your Acting Gene.

Some actors may have had that constant celebration of their Talent while others have had to discover their potential on their own. Whether you're ACTOR A, ACTOR B or somewhere in between, you need to know that if you have the Talent to act, you can have a career as a successful actor. Regardless of where you've come from and where you are now, I can help you mold that Talent into a career.

First, you have a big choice to make.

To act or not to act

Do you want to use your Talent for a career? Keep in mind that the life of an artist isn't an easy one...that is especially true for actors trying to make it in film and television. It is a life filled with rejection, hard work and disappointments. That's not to scare you, it's simply the truth. Those who pursue acting often struggle financially and have to overcome a number of other Obstacles (more on that in Section Two). I've heard actors, both struggling and famous, who wonder what their lives would have been like if they had pursued something other than acting.

As I stated earlier, acting is a gift. You have the choice of whether or not to use that gift. So you could say, "While I acknowledge and appreciate this gift, I choose not to act." Let me tell you there's nothing wrong with that choice. We all know people -- friends, family, co-workers, neighbors -- who have the Talent to sing, dance or act, but never pursued their Talent as a career.

Think back to any community theatre show you saw as a kid. There was always someone in the cast who really shined. They either had a phenomenal voice or terrific acting instincts or both, but they weren't *professional* actors. Rather, they were accountants, lawyers, secretaries, doctors, stay-at-home-moms, etc. They might have dipped their toe in the performing arts, but they never jumped in with both feet. They probably could have had a professional acting career, but they chose not to (for whatever reason). Just because a person has a Talent, it doesn't mean that they necessarily need, want or have to make a career out of it.

For many of you, the choice of whether or not to act is a simple one...you HAVE to do it. There is nothing else you can do or think of doing other than acting. You feel it in your heart, your soul, your bones. Being an actor is your calling.

ACTING IS A CRAFT

Just like any other craft (carpentry, painting, music) or any sport (hockey, tennis, golf), acting needs to be learned, studied, practiced and mastered. You need to put your time, energy and passion into nurturing that acting craft, personalizing it, perfecting it and performing it to the best of your ability. That work never stops, even as you achieve success. Many of today's most accomplished actors still work with an acting coach. The point is, you can only *begin* learning, you can never *stop* learning. You will never stop working at your craft.

There are a lot of people who come to Hollywood dreaming to be a star. And that's okay; I say, "Hey, dream big dreams!" But those actors who think that acting is easy, and that they don't need to study their craft are in for a rude awakening and a rough road ahead.

That's not to say that I haven't seen that rare example of an actor with innate acting ability and no training step right off the bus and right into a job...but it does not make for a career. Raw Talent will only get you so far. You can't last in this business without building your acting skills, without proper acting training.

I know you've heard stories of those actors that have had success without a lot of training or experience.

You've heard the stories of how Chris Klein got discovered in a Nebraska high school to co-star in the film *Election,* or how Topher Grace went from a high school musical to *That 70's Show,* or how Will Smith went from being a rapper to starring in his own TV show, *The Fresh Prince of Bel-Air.*

First of all, these actors were fortunate to get on-the-job training, but they and their stories are few and far between. It's true that these actors got their lucky break early on in their careers, but not one of them sat back and relied on their initial success. Their raw Talent enabled them to get their first job, but then they worked hard to sustain their career. With each role, they challenged themselves, honed their skills and didn't rely on their raw Talent alone. That's why they continue to have successful careers.

Don't jump in too soon!

I know everyone wants to throw themselves into auditioning as soon as they get to Hollywood. It's my strong belief that actors should *not* audition until they have sufficient training. Auditions are for actors who have studied acting and are ready to showcase their Talent in a professional arena.

While auditioning is an opportunity to act, and you can learn many things from auditioning, learning that you need acting class shouldn't be one of them!

I meet many actors who haven't yet trained or studied acting but who are already going out on auditions. Although they may have representation and show great potential or even star quality, they are usually unprepared to tackle professional auditions... and the outcome can be disastrous. I mean, would you ski down a mountain before taking skiing lessons? I hope not!

There are many managers and agents who send actors out on auditions who have yet to set foot in an acting class. In their excitement, they want to show off their new find, get feedback and even motivate the new actor. I will openly admit that when I was an agent, I was guilty of this from time to time. That's not to say that we haven't seen successes in booking brand new actors. But in the long run, it's usually those untrained actors who have booked jobs before they were ready that suffer the consequences.

I'm an actress now

When I was an agent in New York, there was a 17-year-old girl I discovered in a mall. I'll call her Anna. At such a young age, she had a maturity about her. She knew who she was, which made her self-assured and confident. She had a great look -- edgy but pretty. Even though she never had formal training, she had raw Talent. After Anna did a reading for me, I could tell that she had the Acting Gene and enough self-awareness to understand the material. So I decided to represent her.

I got her into acting class, found her a headshot photographer and started to submit her for commercials. The first one she auditioned for, she booked. She was flown to Los Angeles to shoot the commercial. The director liked her so much that a few weeks later, he auditioned her again and she booked another job. She was once again flown out to Los Angeles to shoot a commercial. For a while, she thought all commercials were filmed in L.A.!

A film breakdown came out looking for a teenage girl who was tough, smart and pretty. Although this was a lead film role, I pitched Anna to the casting director. I told him that Anna was a new actress with no formal training, just two commercials under her belt and a couple acting classes. He brought her in anyway and auditioned her. He said she was "a natural." Weeks later, after a few callbacks, Anna booked the job.

It was a major studio film. Not only did she book the movie, the studio signed her for a three picture deal! Plus, the movie was being shot in Hong Kong. It was the perfect Cinderella story, right?

The movie shoot went well for Anna. After filming, she came back to New York to visit me at my office accompanied by the film's lead, a popular '80s teen star...who was also now her boyfriend. As Anna sat there with her head down, he told me that she was going to leave me to sign with his agent at ICM. She meekly picked her head up and said goodbye. And then they left.

After Anna's film came out to moderate success, she went on to shoot her second film. This one apparently didn't go so well. A few weeks into the shoot, I found out she was fired. I heard that she required too many takes, that she had no technique, and the director felt she wasn't connecting to the character. It seems that the raw, untrained Talent that drove her through her first film was not enough to carry her through the second. At the age of 20, Anna was fired and replaced.

Five years later, when I had moved to L.A., I was having lunch and Anna was my server. She greeted me with a big hug. When I asked how she was doing, Anna proudly announced, "I'm an actress now." She said she was studying her acting technique, taking classes and auditioning again. We talked about what she had learned from her experience and the mistakes she made. A year later, I saw her as a series regular on a TV show.

Don't just talk -- act!

In this business, agents, managers and casting directors refer to untrained actors as being "green." Being green means being a novice, a newbie, not a professional yet. Every actor at the beginning stages of their career is "green." Positively speaking, it means you have potential, but you just need to study more. The problem is, too many actors go on auditions or even take on jobs when they're still green.

Many actors think that if they go on enough auditions, they won't be "green" anymore. Being told that you're green on a continual basis will not only jeopardize your relationships with agents, managers and casting directors, it will also take a toll on your confidence level.

If your career is a house, your acting training is your foundation. Without a good, solid foundation, your house will fall down. It won't take an earthquake to bring it down; all you'll need is a few tremors to make it crash.

The best way to build your foundation is through study and practice...and that's where acting class comes in. For an actor, there is nothing more interesting, invigorating and stimulating than being in an acting class.

In acting class, you get a chance to study with other actors who share the same interests and desires. In Los Angeles, you get to study alongside actors who are actually working in film and television, actors who are in the process of making it or those who have made it.

The rest of this chapter will provide you with practical steps you can take to improve your Talent. Whether you're a rookie in the beginning stages of working your craft or an actor with some experience, this chapter will lay out what you need to know to get started, to challenge yourself and to keep the Talent ball rolling.

PRACTICE, PRACTICE, PRACTICE

There are some basic acting classes that all actors should take when they're first getting started as well as classes for actors who already have some training.

There are many wonderful acting studios in Hollywood. Different teachers and techniques will offer new perspectives on developing your skills. You can find an acting studio or coach by simply doing research: websites, asking other actors, recommendations from agents and managers, auditing classes, or reading resource books such as "Acting is Everything" by Judy Kerr.

You must find an acting class that you feel comfortable in, yet challenged. A good acting class will help you develop your imagination, sense memory, emotions, timing, voice and speech, all the while allowing you to create more complex characters and discover new and original ways to enhance the text.

Taking an acting class, though, isn't enough: You have to do the work. In my class, regardless of how talented an actor is, I can tell the ones that practice and the ones that don't. When I work with the actors that do practice, I see a commitment and a constant improvement. That creates a hunger within and makes them better actors. For us acting coaches, it's much more fulfilling to coach an actor who's practiced, rehearsed and fully committed to their scene or assignment.

When you do practice on a continual basis, you will reach peaks in your craft. When you reach those peaks, you "arc" in your acting work. I always encourage actors to set and reach small goals in their acting. As a coach, I watch for specific moments that mark their growth, where you can see the actor blossom and get closer to their potential. I call this "**arcing**" (ark-ing), and it's a word that you'll see throughout this book. It's important for an actor to continue to arc in their work. Every time you arc in your craft you simply get better and better as an actor.

Acting class should be fun, but it also should be challenging. There will be times when you will feel lost, frustrated and even overwhelmed. Just know that's all part of the learning process and your development as an artist. That's part of the challenge.

Find an acting coach you can trust, one who understands you, who "gets" you. Find a coach who believes in your potential to be a working actor. Find someone who will push your boundaries and challenge you to dig deeper into your emotions and imagination.

Acting Classes

These are some acting classes that every actor should have under his or her belt:

• **Basic Acting Technique:** Here is where you'll learn what I call "the nuts and bolts of acting." These classes are designed to provide actors a safe and encouraging environment to explore their innate abilities, their Acting Gene.

These classes teach you how to access your emotions, open up and develop your imagination, and find your acting strengths and weaknesses. They tend to focus mainly on improvisation work and "being in the moment." You learn the value of techniques like personal substitutions, character exploration, repetition and sense memory to help you bring depth to your performances.

They provide a foundation for your acting and introduce you to the teachings of the masters like Meisner, Hagen, Adler, Stanislavski, Strasberg, etc. These basic techniques will be your acting core.

• **Scene Study:** These classes take your basic foundation work and apply it to text from plays, movies, comedies, dramas or even original works.

In Scene Study class, actors are given material to break down and perform with critique from the acting coach. They work on their material at home with a scene partner and bring it back each week to perform in class. They typically work on a scene three or four times over the course of a month, offering the actor a chance to dig into the subtleties and nuances of the material.

The goal of Scene Study is to get you prepared to tackle any type of role, as well as work with partners to explore a scene's rhythm, storyline and purpose. Scene Study classes help you explore a character from an in-depth viewpoint, what makes them unique, what drives them. In these classes, you will build a character, a back story and a relationship to other characters. Scene Study will help you explore that character's Want, Obstacles, Intentions, etc. in a scene (see WOFAIM later in this chapter).

• **On-Camera Classes:** Most actors begin their training doing theatre on stage or working in a classroom. If you're pursuing a career in Hollywood, you need to understand the vital differences between working on stage and working on film.

On-Camera classes will help actors tailor their acting to film and television. Beyond simply showing you how to "hit your mark," these classes will help you bring your acting techniques to the small (and big) screen by being more specific and internal. Working on camera often asks you to be "still" while having a strong emotional inner life. These classes teach you that good film acting happens "all behind the eyes."

In On-Camera classes, actors are often given scenes to perform (mainly from TV and film scripts), which are taped and critiqued by the coach. On-Camera classes offer actors the most true-to-life experience of acting on set.

• **Cold Reading:** When auditioning, more often than not, you will be cold reading. This class is vital to any new (and experienced) actor. They are designed for actors who already have basic technique and scene study training. Because of the nature of cold reading, the actor's technique is put to the test.

Cold Reading classes will help the actor take his or her basic acting mechanics and bring them to a script quickly and efficiently, helping them create an impressive performance. They teach you how to easily lift the words off the page, while staying in the moment with your scene partner.

In these classes, actors are given scripts and usually no more than 20 minutes to prepare. Teachers will provide them with techniques to help them find a character, analyze a script, and make the right choices to give a solid read…quickly. Cold Reading classes morph together your acting instincts and acting technique to help you succeed when you go on auditions.

• **Auditioning Technique:** Auditioning should (and ultimately will) become your main job in L.A. You need to be comfortable in the room from the moment you say hello to the second you say goodbye and all the acting in between. Building upon your acting foundation, scene study and cold reading skills, there are also specific techniques to auditioning that will help you get the role.

Auditioning classes will help you learn how the audition process works. Further, teachers will help you break down audition material (in just a few minutes), find characters quickly and get you ready to walk confidently into any casting office.

In Auditioning classes, you will learn what types of roles you would be called in for and how you can bring your innate Talent and acting abilities to those roles.

Auditioning classes teach actors to make strong choices and trust their instincts as well as integrate their own unique personality into their work. These classes will teach you to be confident in your choices. They will also prepare you for the unexpected, such as a casting director giving you an adjustment, a poor reading partner, or a director suddenly asking you to read for another role. The purpose is simple: to book the job.

• **Comedy:** The art of comedy is considered the most difficult of all the entertainment genres, but if you do it well, you'll have an advantage.

Comedy classes will show you that comedy is much more than witty one-liners and running into walls. There are specific rhythms, styles, techniques and characters that make comedy work...and not just in sitcoms. With television integrating comedy into their dramas (the "dramedy"), comedy classes are becoming more and more of a necessity for the well-rounded actor.

In Comedy classes, actors will learn to tap into what I call The Funny Gene. They will learn to identify different types of jokes and deliver them with comedic precision, i.e. "Triplets," and "The Turnaround."

Comedy classes focus on the science of this genre and how all these techniques must work in harmony with a well-written script and character archetypes that have proven to be successful over the years.

To help you prepare, I suggest reading my first book, "**The Eight Characters of Comedy: A Guide to Sitcom Acting and Writing**," which many casting directors recommend and other acting programs throughout the country are utilizing as a textbook for teaching comedy.

• **Improvisation:** Many acting professionals consider improvisation the purest form of acting because it's the most real, whether it's comedy or drama. There's no script, only guidelines; no written characters, only the actors and the character choices and circumstances they bring to the performance.

For many actors, improvisation is the *scariest* form of acting. A solid improvisation class will help you stay in the moment and think and feel as your character would while relying on only your own instincts.

There are several improvisation schools in L.A., all focused on pushing your boundaries and keeping you on your toes. That's good experience to have for when casting directors, directors or even other actors throw you curve balls in class, the casting room or on set.

• **Commercial:** As much as I'm sure you would all love to book a big film or TV show right away, the reality is that you are more likely to get your start by doing commercials. You should know how to do them…and yes, there are specific techniques to commercial acting.

Commercial classes will teach you how to be…well, you! For commercials you really won't stretch (acting-wise) too far beyond your look or personality as advertisers are looking for *real* people to sell their products. That's not to say you won't learn to be a better actor in commercial class. They are a great place to integrate who you are with your acting ability.

Commercial classes will help you highlight *your* personality and bring a memorable presence and performance to each audition. Further, they will teach you how to "slate," read commercial copy, and work within the confines of the camera. A good commercial class will also help actors prepare mentally, take "smart" risks and be ready to change a performance in case the director wants to see something else.

• **Voice and Speech:** These classes will help you speak clearly and powerfully. As an actor, your voice is one of your most important tools and there are ways to support it, train it, and use it to give a commanding performance. Coaches will teach you more than just vocal exercises and tongue twisters to help keep you articulate.

Using renowned techniques like Linklater, Alexander, Skinner and Barry, these classes will also teach you breathing exercises, warm-ups and different ways you can stretch your mouth, loosen up your diaphragm and utilize your voice more effectively. The goal is to integrate your voice and speech as extensions of yourself and your acting.

These classes will also help you lose your accent. Sure, there will be times when a casting director will be looking for a New Yorker, a Southern Bell or a Latin Lover, but not always. Having a strong accent can limit you.

• **Movement Class:** As an actor, your body and presence are a major source of expression. Movement classes help an actor connect their body with their minds and emotions. They teach you how to be comfortable with how you move. These classes offer exercises that will help you develop a more athletic and agile disposition as well as a confidence in how you carry yourself.

• **Others:** If you can dance, take dance classes. If you can sing, take singing classes. If you're interested in puppetry…you get my point. Essentially, you want to take as many classes as you can to constantly push your Talent, broaden your range and skill set and make yourself a more well-rounded actor.

Actor's Journal

As you go through all your acting classes, it's important to keep all the techniques, information, discoveries, tips, revelations and personal work you accumulate in a notebook.

Your **Actor's Journal** is important in your acting process. It will serve as a constant reference guide of all your acting work. In your journal, you should write down notes from your acting coaches' lectures, performance feedback and any thoughts you have about the work you did in class.

In your Actor's Journal, you should always write down the following:

- Acting technique exercises that work for you
- Personal substitutions
- Imagination exercises
- Strong intentions that work for you in a scene
- Sense memory work
- Character work, including histories and personality traits
- Discoveries and revelations you find in your material
- Any pieces of advice from your teacher that you find helpful

The Actor's Journal is your notebook, workbook and even your personal diary. You should write down personal mantras, affirmations and inspirational quotes you find. It should be used for more than just your class work; it will also be your own personal acting career information guide, where you'll write down things like names of casting directors, audition information, contacts and anything and everything else you learn (or need) in your pursuit of a career.

Your Actor's Journal should feel personal. It's not only a collection of notes and lectures and materials, it's also your intimate thoughts and reflections on your craft and career. Be prepared to go through a few notebooks a year and make sure to safeguard them.

My Acting Technique: WOFAIM

In acting class, you will learn many different techniques that will help you grow as an actor. In my class, I teach a method that combines many different teachings into a technique that is effective for class work, auditions and even work on the set. I call it **WOFAIM**.

WOFAIM is an acronym that encompasses these basic acting techniques. It is a tool that an actor can use to examine, break down and personalize any material. Pay attention to the words I use in this section as they will come up throughout the rest of the book. Without further ado, let me show you how to WOFAIM it.

WOFAIM stands for:

> **W**ant
> **O**bstacle
> **F**eeling
> **A**s If
> **I**ntentions
> **M**oment Before

These are all questions you should ask yourself when first reading a scene or audition sides. Let me break it down even more. Keep in mind, when I say "you," I mean your character.

Want – What do you want? What is your immediate Want in the scene? What is your Objective?

Obstacle – What is the obstacle in the scene that's stopping you from getting what you want?

Feeling – What are the feelings (emotions) you explore throughout the scene?

As If – What is your personal substitution? How do you the actor relate to the experience of the character and their Want? This can come from either your past or your present. Or open up your heart and mind and use your imagination. As if I *what*?

Intentions – Active verbs. What are the active intentions you use in the scene to get what you want? What are your tactics?

Moment Before – What is the logistical moment before and the emotional moment before? What is happening to you physically and emotionally before the scene begins? Where are you coming from?

Ask yourself all of these questions when approaching a scene and it will automatically give you a back story, emotions, intentions and most important, depth to your character. It gets you going before the scene even begins.

I'm going to break down a scene for you and show you exactly how you can use WOFAIM in your work.

EXAMPLE: In this scene, you (your character) want to borrow $300 from your father for acting class. But your father doesn't want to give you the money. He thinks that an acting career is a "waste of time." You need that $300 because you know this acting class will not only help you become a better actor, but will also help get you the next job. Plus, your agent insists you study with this coach. To make matters worse, the class starts this Monday.

What do you **Want**? You want your dad to give you $300.

What is the **Obstacle**? Your dad won't give you the money.

What are you **Feeling**? Anxious, nervous, frustrated.

What is your **As If** (personal substitution)? Well, maybe as an actor, you could identify with this. Has this happened to you in your past? Is this happening NOW? Maybe you've never experienced it. In that case, you need to use your imagination. Remember the time that you needed to borrow your roommate's car to get to an audition and he said "No?" Remember when you needed to borrow your friend's Prada shoes for a hot date and she said "No way?" Essentially, remember a time when you needed something so badly and couldn't get it. You need to personally identify with the character's situation, Want, Obstacles, Feelings and Intentions.

What are your **Intentions**? What active intentions are you using to get your dad to give you $300? What are your tactics? Here are just a few you could use. You could try to persuade, to charm, to guilt, to manipulate, to beg. Any of these could work.

What is your **Moment Before**? Remember this is broken down into two parts. What is your *logistical* moment before? Let's say you're outside the door of your father's study or house and you're about to enter. What is your *emotional* moment before? Well, you are full of anxiety and you're pumping yourself up, trying to build up your courage and overcome your nerves.

Add **stakes** to all of this. I tell my students to look at *three* levels of stakes if they can. It will make the character and his or her Want deeper. In this case, the *stakes* are that you need the money because you don't have it and you need it by Monday. The even *higher stakes* are that this money could get you into a class that could get you a job and will satisfy your agent. The *highest stakes* are that if you get the money, get into class and get the job, you might finally be able to prove to your father that acting is not a "waste of time."

Finally, remember your **thoughts**. As a general note, thoughts are extremely important. They are basically silent thoughts, your subtext, your inner dialogue, what your character is *actually* thinking.

In this example, what are you thinking before the scene with your father begins? What is the thought before you start your dialogue? If you have a good *thought* that matches your character's intention, it will help you rev the engine and come into the scene strong.

Also, what is the thought during the dialogue? Is it the same as what's written? In this scene, the dialogue might read, "Dad, please can I borrow the money?" but what you might be thinking is, "You owe it to me, dammit!" What thoughts might your character be thinking that he or she can't say? Also, *why* are you saying *what* you're saying?

To help you answer that question, and many others, I also developed a script analysis technique called the **Private Eye Method**. These are simple questions that you ask yourself when approaching a script. It's designed to help you search for hints and clues and investigate subtext and circumstances in the material.

Ask yourself these questions when looking at a script or sides:

- How does the scene begin?
- Who are you?
- What's your history?
- Who are the other characters involved (in the scene)?
- What is the time and place?
- What are your current circumstances?
- What is the arc of your character and the arc of the scene?
- How does the scene end?

Answer these questions and WOFAIM a script to the best of your ability, then leave your homework at home. Trust that you've done the homework and you *know* the character's Wants, Obstacles, Feelings, Intentions, etc. Keep all of this with you, stay in the moment and have some fun.

Call to Action Group (CAG)

While WOFAIM and the Private Eye Method are individual techniques that you can use in your acting work, there are group activities that can help you grow in both your craft and career. I will introduce group exercises over the next three chapters. They are designed to enhance, expand and hone your Talent, Confidence and Perseverance skills.

In order to participate, you will first need a group...or what I call a **Call to Action Group (CAG)**. Your CAG should consist of seven people (including you). It's important to find other actors that you can trust, you can be honest with and that are hard-working and dedicated to their craft and their career.

These are people who understand the struggles of getting an agent, the efforts (and expense) in joining SAG, the importance of marketing yourself, the excitement of meeting a casting director and the disappointment of blowing an audition.

Throughout your journey, your CAG will become your practice group, your support group, your marketing group and a whole lot more.

But first, they will be your "acting work" group when facilitating these exercises.

The following exercise is meant to help you access your Talent, use your training and give you an indication of what real acting is like and how powerful it can be. Let me introduce you to The Want Game.

Exercise: The Want Game

The Want Game encompasses a variety of acting techniques all centered on the fundamental core of acting…your Want. However, I also designed the game to touch upon the other WOFAIM elements, including Obstacles, As If and Intentions.

You start by inviting your Call to Action Group over to your place or someplace else that's comfortable and offers some privacy and room for two actors to perform. All you really need is enough space for two actors to simply move around. Set up two chairs facing each other in the middle of that space, a few feet apart. All the other chairs should be set up to face the two chairs in the center.

Everyone in the CAG will get to play The Want Game. Each game takes about 15 minutes. Three players will participate at the same time. Two will actually play The Want Game while a third will act as The Moderator.

The Want Game comes in four Acts. The first Act starts with two players (we'll call them Actor One and Actor Two) sitting in the two chairs across from each other. The Moderator will give each actor a Want from the following list. You'll notice that the

Wants come in pairs. Work with these pairs for the best results. Choose one of these five sets of Wants.

WANTS

#1

ACTOR ONE: *I want you to love me.*
ACTOR TWO: *I want you to leave.*

#2

ACTOR ONE: *I want to borrow money.*
ACTOR TWO: *I want you to get a job.*

#3

ACTOR ONE: *I want you to tell me the truth.*
ACTOR TWO: *I want you to believe me.*

#4

ACTOR ONE: *I want you to help me.*
ACTOR TWO: *I want you to grow up.*

#5

ACTOR ONE: *I want you to take care of me.*
ACTOR TWO: *I want you to back off.*

Actor One will have the first Want (i.e. I want you to love me) while Actor Two will have the second Want (I want you to leave). Once The Moderator assigns the actors their individual Want, they should take a few moments to breathe and relax. When they are ready, each actor should sit up straight in a comfortable position and make eye contact with the other actor. When it looks like they are both ready, The Moderator will have them begin with Act 1.

Act 1: Repetition

In Act 1, The Moderator will only serve as an observer. This game starts very similar to a basic Meisner activity. Both Actors will take turns repeating their individual Wants back and forth to each other. There is no acting in this first part. You should simply state your Want with no intonations, intentions, facial expressions or body movements.

Maintain eye contact with each other and don't think about what you're saying. Simply speak the words to each other and get a feel for your Want. Keep repeating your Want until it becomes second nature. It may feel a little strange and tedious at first, but do your best to connect with the other actor and let the words flow from your lips. Try to stay out of your head. Don't think, just speak.

EXAMPLE:

ACTOR ONE: ACTOR TWO:

I want you to love me.

                I want you to leave.

I want you to love me.

                I want you to leave.

After a few minutes of this repetition, allow yourself to SLOWLY pick up on what the other actor is sending to you. Gradually pick up on your fellow actor's intonations, body language, attitude, speech pattern, facial expressions, positioning, etc. Allow what you observe to affect you. Don't think about it, simply react to it. Connect with your partner and see what organically happens when you allow yourselves to work off each other. Don't force it.

Just keep repeating, while being observant and finding the truth in what you're saying (I promise you, changes will naturally occur).

Act 2: Intentions

As The Moderator observes the two actors staying in the moment, truly connecting with their Want and each other, The Moderator will then add Intentions. These Intentions will give the actors something active to *play*, tactics to help them achieve their Want. If your Intention is "to seduce," your job is to make your partner feel "turned on."

These active verbs will make the interaction between the two actors deeper and more challenging. This type of activity produces a more interesting scene not just for the actors, but also for the observers. Some will only need two or three Intentions to propel them into the scene, while others may need more. The Moderator will choose a few Intentions from the list below and have them ready to give to the two actors as they continue with the exercise.

Intentions:

To attack	To challenge
To charm	To command
To crush	To entice
To mock	To plead
To seduce	To threaten

The two actors will continue repeating their Wants to each other as The Moderator will call out Actor One's name and give them an Intention (to charm). It is the responsibility of Actor One to keep stating their Want while putting an Intention behind that Want.

After Actor One starts to incorporate his or her Intention into their Want, the exercise will shift as Actor Two will organically respond to Actor One's Intention. Then, after a few rounds, The

Moderator will give Actor Two a different Intention (to crush). As Actor Two's Intention starts to play out, Actor One's Intention (to charm) will start to organically change as they react to Actor Two's Intention (to crush).

Let this process naturally evolve. Again, don't try to force these Intentions into your acting. Just keep speaking and reacting until they come naturally.

The Moderator should allow the interaction to unfold until he or she sees the scene is getting stuck or that one of the actors has exhausted that Intention. At that point, The Moderator will then change that actor's Intention by shouting out another one from the list. This also ensures that the actors won't get trapped playing their Want only one way. As The Moderator, feel free to make drastic changes to the Intentions. If Actor One is playing "to charm," change it up and give them "to threaten." If Actor Two is playing "to crush," give them "to plead."

At some point during this phase of the game, The Moderator will ask both actors to stand up, giving them more space as they continue to repeat their Wants and Intentions. This will lead into Act 3.

Act 3: Improvisation

As the two actors stand, repeating their Wants, The Moderator continues to throw out new Intentions. As the scene builds and the actors absorb these new intentions, The Moderator will then yell out, "Improvise."

What I mean by improvise is that both actors continue with their same overall Wants and Intentions, but they are now free to say whatever they like to achieve that Want. As the game progresses to this point, chances are a scenario has formed in each actor's mind. By the time they are on their feet, there is a natural connection to each other, as well as the Want, the Intention and the scenario that has developed. Allowing them to improvise at this point will often unfold a powerful scene.

Note, just like any of the other Acts, you shouldn't force it. Try to stay out of your head and just say what comes naturally. If you can't think of anything to say, simply go back to repeating your Want ("I want you to love me") until something naturally comes out in the moment. Also, remember a basic rule of improvisation is to never negate what your partner is giving you. If they first define you as their friend, lover or boss, then you become that person.

The Moderator allows the two actors to work with each other and play out the improvised scene for a short time. The Moderator then ends the game by shouting, "Scene."

Both actors should take a few deep breaths, let the work they were just doing ease away, sit back down in their chairs, and talk about what they experienced with the rest of their CAG.

Act 4: Reflection and Discussion

Here's a list of things The Moderator should ask the two actors.

- How did the overall exercise feel?
- Did you feel a connection with your partner and did you feel that connection deepen as the scene progressed?
- Did you ultimately identify with your Want?
- Did you feel your Intentions heightened the scene?
- Did they help you achieve your Want?
- Did a specific scenario, real or imaginary (As If) play out in your mind?
- Did your scenario ultimately play out in your improvisation or did you play along with your partner's scenario?
- Did you stay in the moment?
- Did you lose yourself in the scene?

- Did you "check out" or get into your head at any point? Were you able to get back into the scene?

- At the end of the exercise, did you feel excited, invigorated and exhausted.

Take a few minutes to discuss these questions. Then one of the actors who performed will now take over as The Moderator and two new actors will take a seat up front and get ready to play The Want Game.

I use The Want Game as an opportunity for actors to enter what I call the **Acting Zone**, a place where nothing matters except for what is happening in the moment-to-moment interaction between you (your character) and your scene partner? This is what good actors feel after performing well in a scene on a professional set.

The Want Game is a microcosm of everything that good acting encompasses. It's an experience, a chance for you to get into the Acting Zone. The Want Game is also a way for the actor to feel like they're listening and reacting, having a relationship, utilizing active Intentions, all the while staying focused on their Want. It incorporates these major acting techniques and all the major WOFAIM elements you need to be a good actor.

It's not easy, but this experience is what makes acting so challenging, thrilling and ultimately satisfying. And it shows you exactly why it's important to keep working at this craft, keeping it fresh and alive.

Never stop working at your craft

You have to remember that Talent either grows or dies. If you nurture your Talent, it will continue to flourish, but if you stop studying, training and working your Talent, it will lay dormant or just die...and die quickly.

You can't ever simply say, "I'm talented" and that's it. Even if you're Meryl Streep or Robert DeNiro, you still need to work at your craft and constantly challenge yourself. Once you decided you've learned everything you need to know about acting, then you've stopped growing as an actor. If you're serious about acting, you need to work your craft on a daily basis. As I mentioned earlier, you will never stop working your craft and you never stop learning from your craft.

Think of your acting career as a well-balanced diet...your *Career Diet*. And like every well-balanced diet, you have to have protein...and lots of it. In your acting career, Talent is the protein that builds and sustains your acting muscles.

Furthermore, you have to keep *working* those acting muscles or they will become limp and weak; you'll feel the atrophy set in. Think of how it feels when you go to the gym consistently and then suddenly take a few weeks off...when you get back to it, working out gets a lot tougher. It's almost as if you've lost the progress you've made, you've taken a few steps back. It's the same with acting.

You can't take class for a while and then take significant amounts of time off from class or from acting in general. You can't take time off from working those acting muscles. You have to flex and stimulate those muscles as often and as consistently as you can. While class will always be the best place for you to "work out," there are other ways to build your Talent that can compliment your class work.

HOW TO NURTURE YOUR TALENT

Once again, these aren't meant as a substitute for class work, but rather ways to enhance your training along with your class work.

• **Working with a coach:** There is nothing as valuable as the one-on-one experience you can get from working with a professional acting coach. There are a number of renowned coaches in Los Angeles and they can help you prep for auditions as well as work on your specific acting needs. Check out Judy Kerr's book "Acting is

Everything," the publication *Backstage West* and online resources like Now Casting and Actor's Access for reputable Hollywood coaches.

• **Casting director workshops:** Casting director workshops offer a unique opportunity to practice auditioning as well as get some face time with casting directors that may one day hire you. BUT, take note, these CD workshops are not for the green actor. They are only for actors who are well-trained and ready to showcase their work. You are mistaken if you think you can learn how to act from a casting director workshop. Also, don't go into these workshops with the expectation that you're going to get hired or discovered. Instead, use the opportunity to learn about that casting director and the casting process.

• **Theatre:** Working in the local theatre scene is a great way for you to consistently work even when auditions and other projects are slow. The beauty of working in a theatre production is the amount of time spent rehearsing. Theatre shows give you a great opportunity to dig into a character, work your techniques, and practice your craft on a nightly basis. There are several top quality theatre companies in Los Angeles. They're also a great way to meet directors, network, find new friends and build a support system.

• **Watching TV and film:** As an actor, a great way to learn is by watching good acting. Go to the theatre and movies as much as you can, Tivo good TV shows (especially those that you may audition for), and Netflix the great films to see what sets those great actors and their performances apart. A great place to start would be films that feature actors that have been nominated for an Academy Award.

You can't just settle for being good

You need to always strive to be the best. You need to constantly be accessing your Acting Gene and improving on your skills. You need to be acting (in class, on your own, in plays) as much as possible. When it comes to acting in an audition or on set, just being good isn't good enough, you need to be great.

If you have the Talent, you have the opportunity to be great. The way you achieve greatness is through preparation, working your craft, believing in yourself and practicing always.

It's just like being a great athlete. Professional athletes work every single day to make themselves better. Think of Tiger Woods and how many golf tournaments he's won (and how much money he's made over the years). Yet he still competes as often as he can. He's said in interviews, he gets up early almost every morning to work out, arrives at the golf course early to take hundreds of practice shots, and will sometimes take personal weeks to work on a certain part of his game. He is, without a doubt, the best in his business, and maybe the best of all time, and he still works just as hard as he did when he was trying to make his high school team.

That's what you need to do. That's how hard you need to work. That's how you effectively use your Talent. Work it every single day and *want* to work it even more.

The more that you work your craft, the deeper you go, the more fun you have…the better the work and the more you fulfill this portion of what you need to succeed.

Once you are consistently working your Talent, you are ready to go on to the next step.

To be a successful actor, you need to combine your Talent with…Confidence.

CHAPTER 2
CONFIDENCE

In the last chapter, you learned the first Step to Success was Talent, that precious innate ability that -- when combined with technique, training and practice -- will put you on your journey to becoming a successful actor.

Yes, Talent is the foundation, but if you don't believe in yourself or your ability to succeed, you'll *never* make it in Hollywood. If you *do* make it, it won't be for long. To truly realize your potential, you need the second of the Three Steps to Success: **Confidence**.

Having Confidence is having total faith in yourself even when *others* don't. You trust in your abilities and believe that, within reason, you will be able to achieve your goals and fulfill your dreams.

Talent and Confidence go hand in hand. No matter how talented you are, your art, your ability, your craft will always be challenged. Having self-confidence will help you get through those challenges. You'll need this dynamic duo in your corner whether you're performing scenes in acting class, getting an agent, auditioning for a casting director, or working on a television or film set. You need both working in unison as you continue to learn this craft and tackle this career.

In the previous chapter, I told you that Talent was the protein in your Career Diet. Well, if Talent is the protein, then Confidence is the *carbohydrates*. Just like in any diet, there are good carbs and bad carbs. Bad carbs -- like cakes, cookies and chips -- make you feel bloated, lethargic and just plain...yucky. Good carbs, like grains, beans and fruit, power you up and fuel you with the energy you need. That's what Confidence can do for your career.

Confidence is more emotional

Of the Three Steps to Success, Confidence is the most emotionally based, meaning it applies directly to you and your feelings of self-worth and self-assurance. That's what makes it tricky. The way you feel about yourself, present yourself and the messages you put out to the world are key ingredients to your success. Only those who feel sure about themselves, their Talent and their intentions will be successful.

Unlike Talent, Confidence *isn't* something you have to be born with in order to possess (although there are those entering this world with a higher level of self-esteem). For the most part, Confidence is something that is *learned*. Many learn it growing up while others learn it as adults.

Either way, building Confidence and sustaining it is not always easy, especially in a business where you deal with rejection, disappointment and second-guessing on a continual basis.

No matter how much Talent you have, you will experience a lot more rejection than you will success, at least initially. That rejection will often feel personal…and you will *take it* personally. It will make you feel sad, angry and defeated. Confidence, more specifically Confidence in your Talent to act, will help you deal with those feelings and keep you and your career moving forward.

However, Confidence isn't something that just magically appears. Building self-confidence is something you have to work at…daily. The best way for an actor to find Confidence in their Talent is to do the work, whether it's acting class, performing on stage, meetings, going on auditions, or being on a set. Confidence in your Talent and your potential to succeed is found in both accomplishments and disappointments. We learn Confidence through our achievements as well as our failures.

Before I help you build and maintain your Confidence, first we need to assess how much Confidence you have and where it came from.

WHERE DOES CONFIDENCE COME FROM?

You'll see that your Confidence comes from a mix of nurture/ nature -- what you're born with combined with your upbringing -- with some other factors mixed into the pot.

If our DNA determines everything from color of hair to disposition to personality traits to specific talents, then it probably also influences our level of Confidence. Therefore, some children are born a little more outgoing while others enter this world a bit more reserved.

Once again, using a 1 - 3 scale similar to the Talent chapter, let's rate your Confidence level, both what you were born with and how it changed growing up. Again, the point is to look at where you began to determine how much Confidence you have and where you need to grow. Remember, if you're having trouble looking back, don't be afraid to ask your parents or whoever raised you for help.

Confidence Scales:

The Instinctual Years (birth - five years old)

1 Rating: You had very little instinctual self-assurance. You were quiet, shy and reserved, perhaps even a loner. You were hesitant to play with other children or to take part in activities. You had to be pushed to participate. You were afraid to complete tasks (or even start them) because you were afraid of failing.

2 Rating: You were outgoing, the first one to run over to the kids on the playground. You were more curious and that made you more daring. But you were also content to keep to yourself at times. You learned how to walk and talk early, maybe slowly, maybe quickly... but you were proud of yourself for each accomplishment. You were not afraid to take initiative in whatever you were doing.

3 Rating: You were a born leader. You excelled at activities because you were confident in your abilities. You took pride in your accomplishments. Even as a toddler, you were the dominant one in the group. You walked and talked early, showed signs of being decisive, bold and always curious. You could be stubborn and precocious but you believed in yourself and what you were doing.

As with Talent, how much Confidence you have as a small child can change (sometimes significantly) as you go through childhood and into your teenage years. Once again, use the scale to assess how much Confidence you had growing up.

The Formative Years (**six years old - late teens**)

1 Rating: You were shy around other kids and were more content to be on your own. As a teenager, you probably kept to yourself; you were the loner or the outsider of the group. You perhaps lacked the Confidence in yourself to make friends. You might not have had a desire to participate in school activities because of your shyness. You might have found comfort in your solitude.

2 Rating: As a child, you were outgoing enough to follow the pack, but not necessarily lead. As a teenager, you found a small group of friends and got involved in some activities, perhaps to fit in. You went to dances, played sports, performed in school plays, and even had a job. The more you got involved and participated, the more your Confidence started to grow. You didn't necessarily stand out, but you were confident enough with yourself to pursue your dreams and goals.

3 Rating: As a child, you felt self-assured. You made friends easily. You loved to work. You ran lemonade stands, had a paper route, put on shows or organized neighborhood games and clubs. As a teenager, you were the star of the football team, head cheerleader, president of the student council, voted "Most Likely To Succeed." You not only starred in but also directed and produced school plays.

Those with a real high dose of Confidence also may have found some limelight in the arts. You were child stars, dancers, artists, musicians, writers. You didn't really care how you were perceived by others because you were completely and totally confident in yourself and what you did.

Where do you fit in on both of these scales? Did you move up or move down the scales when growing up? Were you a 1 on the Instinctual Years scale that grew into a 2 on the Formative Years scale? Were you a 2 that grew into a 3? Or were you born a 3 on the Instinctual Years scale that slipped down to a 2 on the Formative Years scale?

The even bigger question is *why* you moved up or down that scale. There are many things throughout your life that will affect your Confidence level. Life constantly presents challenges as well as opportunities that will significantly impact how much Confidence you have. Whereas accomplishments and invigorating challenges will boost your Confidence, negative events, medical misfortunes and personal traumas can drain your Confidence.

Like Talent, how your Confidence is initially shaped, and how you maintain your Confidence throughout your life, is mainly influenced by your upbringing.

Confidence comes from your upbringing

Even if you were born overtly confident, that can be suppressed by family circumstances and influences. The opposite is true as well: a shy child can come out of his or her cocoon with the right encouragement, guidance and support. How our parents raised us, what they instilled in us (or didn't instill in us) gives us a pretty good idea of where we stand now and how we need to grow.

Are you ACTOR A or ACTOR B?

ACTOR A: When growing up, were your parents nurturing and supportive? Did they instill in you a strong sense of self-worth? Did they teach you to believe in yourself? Did they encourage you to take risks and try new things? Did they reward you for accomplishing goals?

Or

ACTOR B: When growing up, did you have parents who, because of their own life circumstances, couldn't be there for you? Did your parents lack the time, the know-how, the parental skills or the energy to be there for you? Or did they simply not know how to instill in you a feeling of self-worth?

If you picked ACTOR A, then you are very fortunate. Your parents have given you a solid foundation. It's a blessing that needs to be recognized. Those of you entering this business with a higher level of Confidence usually have less fear. You are often self-assured, daring and direct about your potential. You usually have the courage to risk embarrassment because you believe you will ultimately achieve success. And that's a very good beginning.

If you picked ACTOR B, you probably have a lower level of Confidence. You might feel hesitant, more reserved and insecure. Generally speaking, you tend to have a lot of self-doubt about achieving your Want and you're fearful of taking risks. When you do take risks, you endlessly question your decisions. Growing up, your parents weren't able to give you the support you needed and that's unfortunate (they did their best, you must acknowledge that and then move on).

The good news is, as adults, you have the ability to *change*. You can improve your feelings of self-worth. You can raise your Confidence level. Just knowing that you want to be an actor, declaring it and moving to a new city is the sign of a courageous person. With courage comes Confidence. And *that's* a very good beginning.

Acting Confidence

You should now have at least an idea of how much Confidence you possess. When it comes to Confidence in your Talent, however, there's a catch. Regardless of whether you are ACTOR A, ACTOR B or somewhere in between, you will need to work on a whole new level of Confidence: what I call, **Acting Confidence**.

This Acting Confidence applies specifically to your creative instincts, training, artistic inspiration and the feelings you have about your art and your abilities. Confidence in this ability (or the lack thereof) also translates to your career as an actor.

You are embarking on a professional career, an artist's path where anything can and will happen, where you have to expect the unexpected. No matter how confident or unconfident you are, as an actor you WILL face new situations and experiences that will test both your acting abilities and your Confidence in those abilities. You will need to establish and maintain even more Confidence to get you through these acting career challenges. You'll need to learn how to regulate your self-esteem and keep it balanced as you go forward with your career.

Just like building your Talent is a constant daily process, so is building your Acting Confidence. But there are some specific things you can do to help yourself become more self-assured. The rest of this chapter will not only show you the places both general Confidence and Acting Confidence come from, but also how you can apply these lessons to your own ability and even your life.

YOU CAN BE CONFIDENT

When it comes to building your Confidence, it all starts with *you*. You are the one who will ultimately decide if you are worthy enough to have a career. You are the one who has the control over your self-esteem in both your life and your acting career. You are the only one with the power to lift your Confidence.

Whether your Confidence level is high or low, I ask you to take this journey with me from the very beginning. For those entering with a higher level of Confidence (ACTOR A), the following exercises will not only reinforce your Acting Confidence level, but also heighten your overall self-esteem.

For those of you with a lower level of Confidence (ACTOR B), you will start building upon what you have from the ground up. I will show you how to gain and preserve your Confidence on your career path.

For those that struggle with very low self-esteem and low self-worth, I suggest to first seek help and guidance through therapy and counseling. Therapy is a way to learn about yourself and why you do the things you do. Therapy can only make you more evolved, enlightened and self-aware, which makes for a better actor and a better human being. These exercises are by no means a substitute for professional help. Hopefully, though, they will get you on the road to believing in yourself.

We all need affirmation

When I was an agent in New York, I found that many of my young clients lacked the Confidence they needed to book the job. Even though they were trained actors, something inside them (some negative voice or event) made them second-guess themselves, which interfered with their acting work. As much as I told them to "believe in themselves," the seeds of self-doubt kept creeping into their conscious minds. I decided to take action. So I taught them the power of **Affirmations**.

Affirmations are positive thoughts you speak out loud. They are designed to alter the way you think and feel about yourself. Affirmations invigorate you, encourage you and pump you up when you feel uninspired, deflated or defeated. There's a lot of power in "thoughts"...positive ones and negative ones. Before I get to the positive ones, let me talk about those destructive negative thoughts that attack your Confidence level. Let me show you how to get rid of them.

Negative thoughts begin in your subconscious. They were planted there by past negative experiences or events. You could say your negative thoughts are a by-product of your negative experiences. These negative thoughts are formed into damaging statements that you say to yourself or speak out loud (sometimes in front of others):

"I'll never be happy."
"I look ugly."
"I feel unworthy."
"I'll never be a good actor."
"I'll never succeed."

Do any of those negative thoughts or statements sound familiar? Are they part of your vocabulary? The problem is, when said often enough, your subconscious mind believes these negative thoughts or statements to be true. They *become* true only because you consciously believe them to *be* true. That's how the vicious cycle of self-doubt begins and never ends. It's these negative thoughts that prevent you from achieving your career goals. Here's what you need to do:

• First, you need to consciously stop planting those negative thoughts in your mind.

• Second, you need to stop saying them out loud (be diligent in catching these negative thoughts).

• And third, you have to reprogram those negative thoughts that have already taken up residence in your subconscious. The only way to reprogram them is to first change them in your conscious mind.

Exercise: I am...

Your first Affirmation is meant to uncover your negative thoughts and turn them into positive thoughts. Choose a negative statement you find yourself saying and change it to a positive statement. Make sure you start your positive statement with the words, "I am." Those two words are very powerful and serve as a command meant to lead you to a positive outcome. Make sure you write down your positive statement in your Actor's Journal.

For example, using the negative statements I mentioned earlier:

If you say, "I'll never be happy," change it to **"I am happy."**

If you say, "I look ugly," change it to **"I am beautiful."**

If you say, "I feel unworthy," change it to **"I am worthy."**

If you say, "I'll never be a good actor," change it to **"I am a good actor."**

If you say, "I'll never succeed," change it to **"I am succeeding."**

Positive affirmations need to start with a positive declaration. Look at what you wrote down and say it out loud. The more you say it, the more you'll train both your conscious and subconscious mind to believe it.

As in acting, make sure those words, and the feelings behind them, come from somewhere deep inside you. Concentrate on what you're saying and feel the negative thought leave your mind and body as you let the positive one in. Each time you say it, believe that you are truly letting go of your negative thought and the feelings that are attached to it. Believe in the positive words you are saying.

Exercise: I am good enough to be great.

Of course, remnants of your negative thoughts will still linger. Let me show you how to counter those nagging negative thoughts with an even more positive thought.

This next Affirmation will be all-encompassing to your life as well as your career. Once again, write this down in your Actor's Journal:

I am good enough.

Now clear your mind, close your eyes, take a breath, and say it out loud five times:

I am good enough.

As you repeat this Affirmation to yourself over and over, some flashes of a past negative event may play out in your mind like a home movie. You might become emotional as this negative experience runs through your mind. You might see someone telling you that you're not good enough, not smart enough, not good-looking enough or that you're too fat, too skinny, too small, too tall. Or the event could have been much more specific, like you forgot your lines in a play, which left you feeling embarrassed or humiliated. It's something that left a deep scar.

Acknowledge this negative event, and the thought and emotions that go with it. Exhale and let the negative thought start to evaporate. Counter this negative thought with a more passionate, positive thought. Open your eyes and say it again:

I am good enough.

Say it as many times as you need to wash that negative thought away. Feel it and experience it slipping from your mind. You should feel relief as you allow yourself to be rid of the negative thoughts that surround that negative event. Hear the words come out of your mouth. Listen to that single voice, that single Affirmation. Say it again, say it louder and stronger:

I am good enough.

Let's take it one step further. Now, you're going to say it directly to yourself. Walk over to a mirror, look yourself in the eyes, take a deep breath and say:

I am good enough.

Keep saying it until the person staring back at you believes it. Once you feel it in your body and you truly believe that you are good enough, take another deep breath, and say:

I am good enough to be great.

You should feel stronger, exhilarated and more empowered. You have triggered the positive energy that you possess. You should feel a belief building in yourself. You have embraced your potential and you are ready to move forward and be great.

Exercise: I believe in myself.

This next Affirmation will help you believe that you *are* good enough to be great.

Once again, write this down in your Actor's Journal.

I believe in myself.

Then take a breath and say it out loud:

I believe in myself.

Say it again, quietly, to yourself.

I believe in myself.

32

Feel it, own it and live by it. This should become your mantra, part of your morning ritual. Before you brush your teeth, drink your coffee, or pick up your cell phone, you need to look in the mirror and say "I believe in myself" three times.

You will immediately see a difference. You will gain a stronger desire to achieve your Want and you will be more positive about your prospects. Incorporate your mantra into your daily life. Say it to yourself three times before you go to class. Say it before you go into a meeting with an agent. Say it after a rough day before you go to sleep.

I believe in myself.

This Affirmation is especially effective before auditions. It will counteract any prior self-doubt and negative thoughts and statements about failing such as "I'm going to screw up this audition." It's equally as valuable *after* auditions to block any negative thoughts from re-entering your subconscious like "I just screwed up that audition."

Also, to complement this Affirmation, try the following visualization exercise at home or sitting in your car before any audition:

Once again, relax, take a deep breath, and imagine the inside of the casting room. Picture yourself standing in the middle of the room performing your scene with focus, energy, passion and the Confidence that comes with being fully prepared. Picture a casting director, writer, producer and director all sitting across from you, smiling, interested, taking notes and circling your name on their call sheet. As you finish your audition, visualize them smiling, thanking you for your work, and telling you with a wink that they'll be in touch. See yourself walking out of the audition with your shoulders back and your head held high, proud and satisfied with your audition, confident that you did your best.

Visualizing a positive outcome will fuel you with Confidence.

Exercise: I am a confident actor.

In this final Affirmation, I'm going to help you build upon the Confidence you already have. I'm going to help you find something you're confident about and translate that into your acting. I'm going to help you accept that you can be a confident actor.

First, let's find out where else in your life you feel the most confident. Steer it away from acting. Think of something you know you are good at, something that you believe you can do and do well. We all feel confident about something. Do you feel most confident about your relationships, at your job, playing a sport, school work, giving advice, in having sex?

Where are you most confident? Write it down in your Actor's Journal.

I am very confident when I . . .

Let's say you wrote down, "I am very confident when I am driving." That doesn't mean you have to be an expert or a professional racecar driver. It just means that driving is something you feel sure of doing.

In other words, when you drive, you are not fearful of the road or other motorists. You feel relaxed, yet in control. When driving, you are cautious even when you're talking to your passenger, singing along with the radio, or talking on your headset. You feel free, at ease, your thoughts are flowing. You feel confident and the Confidence surges through your body.

Well, that's how you should ultimately feel about your acting, whether it's in classes, auditions or on the set. You should feel comfortable with the material. You should feel at ease in the room. You should feel strong about your intentions. You should feel confident. You should feel like you're a good actor.

I want you to think about that activity, the one that makes you feel confident. Picture yourself doing it in your mind and feel the Confidence rise in you. Attach that powerful feeling to the following words. Write it down and say it out loud three times:

I am a confident person!

Carry that feeling and that positive thought into the classroom, meeting or your next audition. Experience the difference it makes.

Translate those feelings of Confidence into your *acting*. Say it out loud:

I am a confident actor!

As you work on your Confidence in and out of acting class, this mantra will ultimately become your personal truth.

Now you have strong personal Affirmations to work with in gaining Confidence and sustaining it on a daily basis. Take these Affirmations and write them on a Post It. Hang the Post It on your computer, your bathroom mirror, your dashboard or put it in your wallet to always carry with you as a reminder.

I am good enough to be great.
I believe in myself.
I am a confident actor.

WORKING YOUR CRAFT

Many actors ask me, "How can I feel more confident as an actor?"

The answer is simple: Practice your craft.

While mantras and personal growth are a great way to get a start on building up your *overall* Confidence, there is nothing that will help you sustain your *Acting* Confidence like working on your craft. Before you can feel more confident as an actor, you first need to feel more confident about your acting ability.

This is where acting class comes in. In order to be a confident actor, you need to constantly practice your acting techniques: accessing emotions, imagination work, personal substitution, characterizations, etc. You need to always be working on scenes, monologues, improvisations and your cold reading skills. At the end of every acting class, you should leave feeling enlightened, excited and moved. You should walk out of class with a little more Confidence in your craft and in yourself.

Just as acting class will help you develop your Talent, it will also help your Confidence blossom. Acting class is really the point that these two Steps to Success begin to merge together for most actors. Acting class pushes your creative boundaries in a safe environment. Acting class should also be a place where you feel comfortable enough to fail and fall flat on your face -- only to pick yourself up and try again. That's part of an actor's growth. The more an actor grows or arcs in class, the better he or she feels about their individual Talent. Talent and Confidence always work together, whether we're talking acting, singing, dancing…or professional sports.

Acting is like a game of tennis

In my seminars, lectures and acting classes, I talk about how the career of an actor often mirrors the career of a professional tennis player.

Watching two good actors perform an intense, high stakes scene is like watching a wonderful tennis match. The back and forth interplay is what makes for fascinating entertainment.

As each *player* enters the match with a strategy as well as a willingness to change that strategy, each *actor* enters the scene with strong intentions and a willingness to change those intentions…to be in the moment.

Each player is focused and has a specific Want (to win the game), clear Obstacles (their opponents), clever tactics (serves, lobs, backhands) as well as a powerful Moment Before (the stance before the serve).

Like an actor, a tennis player is born with some innate ability (Talent). As the tennis player grows up, there is hopefully a sufficient amount of faith, belief and support from parents, coaches, loved ones, etc. There are also great lessons to be learned from observing other tennis players.

The main way a tennis player gets better, though, is by practicing and believing in themselves. Yes, I'm sure tennis players have mantras too. I'm sure one of them is "practice, practice, practice."

They work with a coach, take lessons, and perfect their techniques: their stance, serve, hand-eye coordination, awareness of the court, hitting style and the anticipation of their opponents' shots. The more they practice their techniques, the more confident players they become.

Eventually, they feel certain about what they've learned and they're ready to play the game. When they first start playing, they don't always win, but they learn from their mistakes and grow from their losses. They pick themselves up to play another game, to keep at it, to win!

When they begin to win, their Confidence level rises and they want to play more. They get a taste of success, which feeds their Confidence. They start challenging better tennis players. Their Confidence drives them, pushes them to be the best they can be. As they get better, they get more confident -- that's the cycle of success.

This is no different for actors. You need to always practice and be ready to play. You need to get an acting coach, take classes, learn techniques and then arc in your progress as an actor. You will train. When you are ready, when you are confident, you will audition. You will walk into any audition unafraid because you are prepared. You are now a trained, professional, confident actor. That's the goal.

OBSERVING OTHERS

Great artists are great observers of life. As actors, we observe people all the time. In order to create authentic, multi-dimensional characters, we model ourselves after others and integrate their personalities into our work. We adopt their speech patterns, intonations and dialects. We observe their behaviors, mannerisms and how they carry themselves. We learn about their hopes and desires, their achievements and failures, as well as their insecurities...and what they're most confident about.

Who in your life is confident? Look to your family, your friends your co-workers. Who walks and talks with self-assurance. Who is direct, decisive and even intrepid? Is it your father, your older sister, your boss, your best friend, your acting coach?

Make sure you're not picking someone who's arrogant. There's a big difference between Confidence and arrogance. People who showcase their self-importance and contempt for others are usually masking insecurities and overcompensating for it by *acting* superior. They are full of false pride...full of bravado! Those with a real sense of Confidence know what they want and *work hard* to get it. That's the kind of person you want to observe.

In your Actor's Journal, write down the person in your life who is the most confident.

Believe it or not, you have consciously or unconsciously studied this person. What makes them confident? What qualities about them do you wish you had? Most likely, these are people who are successful in whatever they do, so how did they achieve that success? Often, these are people that have a specific Talent, ability or skill that makes them successful. You're noticing their Talent as well as their Confidence in their Talent.

There are some things to look for that confident people possess. These are not only personality traits that identify a confident person; they are also personal tasks and challenges that you can work on to help build up your own Confidence level in your career.

What would a confident person do?

A confident person…

• Is open to criticism.

• Sets goals they can attain.

• Will work to accomplish those goals.

• Expects good things to happen.

• Is open to new challenges.

• Is willing to take risks.

• Gets involved.

• Is comfortable in their own skin.

• Speaks authoritatively.

• Experiences their fear and overcomes it.

Understanding, embracing and incorporating these personality traits will not only help you become a more confident person in your acting career, but also in your daily life. Each day, work on implementing these characteristics into your own acting career. Be more authoritative, set goals, challenge yourself, get involved and expect that only good things will happen. Most important, be comfortable with who you are.

KNOWING YOUR TYPE

There's nothing more powerful than an actor who knows who they are and embraces it. As an agent and casting director, when I met an actor with a great sense of self, they would immediately capture my attention. They showed me something that intrigued me, made me want to get to know them better, to see more. There is a power in self-awareness.

Your self-awareness will permeate everything you do, and that's important in your acting as well as your acting career.

Once you know who you are, then you can begin the process of discovering and identifying what kind of characters you play best. Knowing your **type(s)**, and playing it (or them) to the fullest will give you the Confidence you need in your auditions, meetings and career as a whole. More importantly, it will get you the job. It will help you continue to market yourself in this competitive industry. Knowing your type is another tool in the actor's toolbox. The more tools to draw from, the more confident you will become.

Character archetypes

We all know the basic types of characters in films and television: the All-American Boy, Girl Next Door, Lawyer, Computer Nerd, Everyman, etc. Whether you're doing comedy or drama, film or television, you have to know your type, which of these categories you most naturally fit into.

It starts with your appearance, your look. Determining your look and the type that is attached to that look will help you get auditions. This is especially true in commercials. If you look like the All-American Boy or the Girl Next Door, you'll get called in for *those* auditions.

Film and television roles, however, are more multi-dimensional. It's not only your look, but also the complex personality traits that go along with your look, that create authentic characters. Even though your appearance is significant in getting a part, what's equally important is knowing what personality traits you possess that you can bring to that specific character.

For example, a casting director might bring you in because you look like the All-American Boy, but if they wanted this character to be angry and rebellious, could you relate to that frustration and rage? Or if the role asks you to be the kind, sweet Girl Next Door who gets pregnant, can you understand her innocence, naivete and fear? Could you play a powerful, aggressive Lawyer because inside of you is a strong-willed person? Could you play the Computer Nerd because you identify with his intellect and awkwardness? Could you play the Everyman who secretly is a serial killer because you can tap into the dark side of your own personality or imagination?

These TV and film roles can be played many different ways -- it's your look merged with your own personality traits that will make these characters unique and interesting. Your best chance to get the job is to play characters not only close to your look, but also close to your essence, your life experience, your emotional depth and the depths of your imagination.

Building your niche

For many actors coming to Los Angeles, especially those of you who have graduated from formal acting programs, I'm sure you have played many different characters in your acting classes and staged productions.

Acting class is where you take creative risks, push your boundaries, play a broad range of characters, make wild character choices. While that will make you a well-rounded actor, it may also give you the impression that you could book any role...no matter how against your type.

For example, in acting class, a 21-year-old actor can play an 80-year-old character in a scene. They can even perform that older character on stage in a full-length play. But they would never be cast to play that role on television or film. The casting director will get a *real* 80-year-old actor.

When you're doing stage work, you can put on makeup, a wig and alter your appearance. You can change your voice, your costume, your walk and gait to become the "character." On a stage, where the audience is slightly removed, you can get away with that, but not with the intimate close-up of a television or film screen.

Unless you are a crafted, experienced, professional actor like Helen Mirren, Johnny Depp, Cate Blanchett or Philip Seymour Hoffman, chances are, especially at first, you are going to play someone who pretty much resembles *you*. Playing someone you are familiar with inside and out -- yourself -- will automatically instill Confidence where you need it most…in the casting room.

Casting directors know you

Casting directors are "people watchers." They study people. They are very insightful and more often than not, a good casting director has the gift to see beyond an actor's look…they can see an actor's essence.

When a casting director is looking to cast a role, they put out breakdowns to agents and managers looking for actors. They will call an actor in for an audition based on their look, experience and an agent or manager's recommendation.

From the moment the actor walks into the room, the casting director begins to evaluate whether or not they're right for the role. They make their initial judgment based on the actor's appearance, the way they carry and present themselves, and the little chitchat they have with the casting director before the audition.

What the actor does when they perform the scene will either change the casting director's mind or validate their initial assessment. After the actor reads, the casting director will decide if they're right for the role or not. They're looking for a certain "connection" that the actor has to the material, the character they're reading for. That connection can only come from the actor's understanding of the nature of the character and what they instinctually and organically bring to that character.

Actors feel that focusing on only a certain type will limit their auditions and their career. The truth is, defining your type and knowing your niche will make you stand out more and give you more Confidence. *That* will set you apart from other actors. You'll get more auditions that you're right for, and ultimately…you'll work more.

So who are you?

The concept of truly discovering your type is complex and takes time. It's a process. You first need to know who you are as a person and that's not always easy to see. It's difficult to stand back and objectively observe yourself. In order to do that, you need to consciously take note of certain personality traits you possess, traits that make up the essence of *you*.

So let's start there. Write down in your Actor's Journal five adjectives that you think best describe you. Be as honest with yourself as possible. For example:

Eccentric
Exciting
Unpredictable
Funny
Moody

The catch is, who you think you are and what you put out to the world can be two different things. We're going to see if others agree with these specific character traits or if they perceive you differently.

Here is a game that I've been playing in my acting class for many years. It's an exercise that effectively helps actors begin the process of identifying and embracing who they are. It's a good exercise to help you see how others perceive you and how that relates to how you perceive yourself. Let me introduce you to…

Exercise: The Typing Game

Once again, its time to invite over your Call to Action Group for another activity.

Find a relaxed, safe environment to play **The Typing Game**. All participants will need small writing pads (Trait Sheets), pens, water and a place to sit. You will also need a timer and a large pad of paper to hang up for all the participants to see.

Everybody in the group is going to participate. From now on, the player will be referred to as Actor One and the rest of the players will be referred to as The Group. The host goes first.

Actor One leaves the room and gives The Group a few seconds to prepare for the activity. On top of the Trait Sheet, write down the name of Actor One. The timer is then set for five minutes. When The Group is ready, Actor One walks back into the room and sits silently in a chair in front of The Group. Without conversing, The Group immediately writes down on their individual Trait Sheets what they believe is the player's age range in five-year increments (17-22, 20-25, 25-30, 30-35, 35-40 and so on).

Actor One continues to sit in silence for 10 seconds more as The Group writes down their first adjective from the Personality Traits list provided (this list should be written on the large pad of paper for the whole group to see and used as a reference). While I encourage you to use these strong adjectives, you should also feel free to come up with your own.

Personality Traits:

Grounded	Innocent	Insecure
Responsible	Happy	Provocative
Charming	Frustrated	Anxious
Desperate	Smart	Shameless
Lovable	Pretty	Perfectionist
Sweet	Condescending	Articulate
Attractive	Caring	Positive
Educated	Tough	Sarcastic
Fearful	Talkative	Angry
Analytical	Sexy	Sad
Awkward	Smooth	Troubled
Childlike	Perky	Shy
Funny	Aggressive	Distant
Good-natured	Judgmental	Aloof
Moody	Excited	Eccentric
Enthusiastic	Optimistic	Fiesty

Within the five-minute period, Actor One begins to answer the following questions. They may never get through all of these questions (in fact, they may only answer one). That's fine. Actor One should simply use these questions as a guideline to share something about themselves with The Group:

- Where did you grow up and what was it like? (Describe your city, your town, your neighborhood, etc.)

- What was your upbringing like? (Describe the relationship you had with your mother, your father and your siblings).

- Who in you're family were you closest to growing up and why?

- Who are you closest to now and why?

- Who are you most like now?

As Actor One talks, The Group will silently write down four other adjectives, once again from the Personality Traits list or their own. When the timer goes off, Actor One stops talking and The

Group stops writing. Each Trait Sheet should be folded so nobody can see what was written. The Trait Sheets are then collected by Actor One, paper-clipped and put aside. Actor One should not look at what's written on the Trait Sheets; that will come later.

Actor One takes a seat and becomes part of The Group as Actor Two leaves the room. Clear your mind for the next player and follow the same steps.

After every player has participated and all Trait Sheets are collected, the game is over. Take a moment to decompress. Don't discuss the specifics of what was written but feel free to talk about what the exercise felt like...and then say goodbye.

When you are alone, take all your Trait Sheets and spread them out on a table. In your Actor's Journal, write down all your adjectives that you got from The Group. Begin to tally the age ranges and the characteristics. Write down the word and count how many times the other players used that word. You will then take your adjectives and write yourself a character breakdown incorporating as many of those character traits as possible.

Here are examples from three of my students -- Jim, Max and Katie -- followed by my assessment of each:

JIM

Age:
20-25 (1), 25-30 (5)

Adjectives:
Optimistic (6)
Charming (5)
Funny (5)
Good-natured (4)
Hopeful (4)
Jolly (4)
Attractive (1)
Talkative (1)

Breakdown: Jim is an attractive, good-natured guy in his mid-20s, who is sometimes jolly. He is hopeful and very charming to talk to and he has a funny, optimistic approach to life.

Assessment: Having all very similar characteristics appear on your Trait Sheet like Jim (optimistic, charming, funny) is certainly helpful because it's clear what you're putting out there. Jim could get work in commercials. What Jim lacks is depth in his character. I told him he needs to find and work material in class that will help him uncover and unleash the other side of his personality. He needs to expose his flaws and vulnerabilities (insecure, sad, frustrated) to get work in TV and film.

MAX

Age:

25-30 (1), 30-35 (2), 35-40 (3)

Adjectives:

Shy (3)
Outgoing (3)
Aloof (2)
Desperate (2)
Frustrated (2)
Insecure (2)
Awkward (2)
Self-assured (2)
Smart (2)
Aggressive (1)
Anxious (1)
Caring (1)
Enthusiastic (1)
Judgmental (1)
Lovable (1)
Perfectionist (1)
Positive (1)
Responsible (1)
Tough (1)

Breakdown: Unable to do exercise.

Assessment: Max was unable to write a character breakdown. As you can see in his adjective list, Max had a lot of varying characteristics (shy, outgoing, insecure, self-assured) as well as many single adjectives, "1's."

Having a lot of "1's" on your Trait Sheet signifies that people don't know how to perceive you. That's why Max couldn't do the assignment or build a character breakdown based on the adjectives given to him. Immediately upon seeing his Trait Sheet, Max knew that it was difficult to put these varied characteristics into a character type. Max wasn't surprised. He told me, "My friends *always* have trouble figuring me out." Well, if Max's friends are going to have trouble figuring him out, an agent, manager or casting director most certainly will. Having such a scattered range says to the industry, "I don't know who I am, I don't know what type I am."

I told Max that he needs to understand that he's in the process of discovering himself. He needs to work on figuring out who he is as a person, as well as an actor. The best advice for Max is to work on different types of material in various genres until he finds characters that naturally fit and best showcase the strongest sides of his personality…and then build from there.

KATIE

Age:
17-22 (3), 20-25 (3)

Adjectives:
Attractive (4)
Bright (4)
Charming (3)
Grounded (3)
Over-achiever (3)
Reserved (3)
Vulnerable (3)

Daddy's Girl (2)
Thoughtful (2)
Unsure (2)
Troubled (1)

Breakdown: Katie is an attractive, bright overachiever who strives for excellence in all she does. Her upbringing keeps her grounded and a tad reserved. She is extremely thoughtful of others and a bit of a daddy's girl. At times she can be vulnerable and unsure, but would never let you see it. Beyond her charming demeanor and well-put-together exterior is a world of sadness from her troubled childhood.

Assessment: Great characterizations are layered and finding the characteristics within those layers that you naturally identify with is how you really begin to find your type. The best kind of response in The Typing Game is to have very specific characteristics along with opposing characteristics on your Trait Sheet like Katie. Her personality list shows that she is "grounded," but "vulnerable;" "charming," but "troubled."

Some might be surprised to see some of these "negative" adjectives. However, having these negative personality traits is human, it's universal. It shows you are flawed, which is interesting. Those negatives are actually positives to the inner life of a character...if you can embrace them. Katie's not afraid to show depth in her personality and her work, which will serve her well in the casting room. She has a better opportunity to book. I told Katie to keep exploring and infusing herself into her work.

You need to give up a little of yourself

How you look might not always go along with what your personality says about you. This is very difficult for many actors to accept, especially those new to the business. It's worth repeating: actors have to understand that their look is a defining factor in what roles they'll play. Sometimes you need to give up a certain "look" to play a character type that fits you best.

As an example, a student of mine (I'll call her Sharon) went through a mini-metamorphosis after playing The Typing Game. Sharon didn't know her type. She complained that the industry didn't get what type she was either. She constantly got vague, conflicting opinions from prospective agents and managers of what characters she should play. The good news is that after doing this exercise, she found her *true* character by taking a hard, objective look at herself…and being willing to make a change.

Sharon presented herself as a Paris Hilton type, a "glamour girl," with long, blonde hair extensions, French manicured nails and sexy, trendy clothes. She was going for the chic, club girl look…the kind all the men want in beer commercials.

The problem was…Sharon wasn't a beer girl! She wasn't a Paris Hilton type. She wasn't beautiful by Hollywood standards. She was attractive, but more like the "best friend" type. She was intelligent, very complex, and she had quite a bit of depth.

After Sharon did The Typing Game and tallied The Group's adjectives, she saw some similar personality traits (smart, responsible, reasonable, grounded, straightforward, nurturing). That *was* a strong reflection of who she was and what she most resembled. Interestingly, of the 25 adjectives she received, only a few described her as the glamour girl she thought she was (well-dressed, stylish).

As you can imagine, it was a big awakening for Sharon. Once she was able to acknowledge and embrace her own characteristics, she decided to take a chance and change her look. Gone were the hair extensions, the long nails, the trendy, sexy clothes. She simplified her look and emerged as an intelligent, classy young woman with style and sex appeal. She was ready to tackle the young professional roles and she became a working actress.

The message here is to accept and embrace who you are as a person and as an actor. Search inside yourself, play The Typing Game and find out who you really are…and be comfortable with that. Knowing who you are will help give you the Confidence you need to walk into any agent office, casting room or on any set.

YOUR COMFORT ZONE

Moving to Los Angeles is an overwhelming adventure to say the least. Many actors get through these initial stages of setting up their new life on sheer excitement and adrenaline. They have such hope, desire and optimism as they embark on this journey, that their first three months is a whirlwind, a blur of organizing, making calls, driving around the city and shopping at IKEA. It's thrilling!

It can also be terrifying. Many actors uproot their lives and move to L.A. without really knowing anyone. Many don't even have a place to live or at best they have a *temporary* place to live. For the most part, they have left behind their schools, jobs, family and friends...all that is familiar to them. They might not have a support group or that older, wiser, more experienced person that they can trust. They are trying to take on a new city, a new job, a new career, a whole new life...and they are often going into it blind, without the security and stability of their **Comfort Zone**.

Finding a new Comfort Zone within the first three months in Los Angeles is vital to getting settled, staying positive, and preparing to embark on your new journey. It's also important for maintaining your Confidence. You need to feel comfortable, to find your new Comfort Zone as quickly as you can. Here are some essentials that will help you begin a new life in Hollywood.

Eight ways to build your Comfort Zone:

1. Get Judy Kerr's book "Acting is Everything."
2. Get a place to live.
3. Get a car.
4. Get a job.
5. Get into acting class.
6. Get a support group.
7. Get a TV.
8. Get a mentor.

1. Get Judy Kerr's book "Acting is Everything." This wonderful book will give you all the practical information you need to get started in Los Angeles: where to live, where to work and where to play. Judy's book lays out anything and everything you need to know about the acting business. Judy's inspiring, maternal, reassuring voice shines through the pages, making the daunting journey a little easier. "Acting is Everything" will be a logistical and essential roadmap to life in Hollywood.

2. Get a place to live. Find a place you can call *home*. It needs to be safe, someplace you feel the most at ease. Your life in L.A. is going to be hectic and draining at times. Whether you live by yourself or with a roommate, you need a place you can come back to in order to relax and recharge. For your career, this will also need to be a home base of operations with a desk, a computer, privacy and a space where you can rehearse your acting scenes. Get a place to live that is affordable, comfortable and near Hollywood

3. Get a car. You need a car in Los Angeles. Riding a bus won't get you where you need to be in the time you need to be there. The city's too spread out and you will need to go from the Valley to Hollywood to Santa Monica to Beverly Hills...sometimes all in one day. The car should have four wheels, an engine...and a warranty. Sure, it probably won't be the latest model, but it will have character. When you are a successful actor, you will look back and remember it as your "first L.A. car." It will have a special place in your heart as a reminder of your starving artist days.

4. Get a job. This is not a career job, it's a survival job. I'll tackle this issue more in Section Two, but for now, just know that your survival job should offer you enough money to do just that... *survive.* Find yourself a job (or jobs) that give you flexible hours so you can concentrate on your acting career. Although I advise coming to Los Angeles with at *least* some kind of savings...it won't last. You need to get a survival job right away so you have enough money to pay the rent, living expenses and acting class tuition.

5. Get into acting class. Along with fulfilling the basic need to study your craft, acting class is a great way to meet other actors. Within any acting class, you will immediately find new friends, some who will be friends for life. You will also learn more about the business from both newbies and actors who have been here awhile. You will make industry connections...many actors find their agents through other actors.

You should find an acting class that has 10 to 15 people. In a smaller group, it will be easier to meet people. Also, find a class that periodically offers group or partner assignments so you work outside of class together. That way, you're not only learning your craft, you're also forming an acting support group that will help build your Comfort Zone and your Confidence.

6. Get a support group. Even if your family is supportive of you becoming an actor, chances are they are not in Los Angeles with you. They may be a phone call, text message or an e-mail away, but they are not physically with you in your everyday activities. As you tackle a whole new set of circumstances, obstacles and emotions, you need to start forming a second family, a family of friends that will become your support group.

Find friends you can go to coffee, lunch, movies or the bar with, friends with whom you can share your life, friends you can laugh with, really talk to and trust. These friends will not only be your emotional support system, they will also be your partners as you explore this new, exciting life in L.A.

Further, some of these new friends may also be actors who could make up your CAG. They will help you deal with the challenges of the craft, the pressures of your career and the turbulent life of an actor in Hollywood. You can form these support groups with other people you find anywhere: in class, at your job, in your apartment complex, workshops, auditions, theatre companies or even Starbucks.

You need to find a support group who will be completely honest and sympathetic to you and your cause. When your Confidence in your acting career is at its lowest, turn to these friends who understand you and what you're going through.

Remember, you're in a town filled with actors who share your same fears, dreams, concerns and goals. That's one of the most thrilling aspects of living in Hollywood. You can befriend the competition and you can actually help each other survive! They will be vital to your Comfort Zone.

7. Get a TV. As discussed in the Talent chapter, watching TV is part of your job as an actor. You need to keep up with shows (and commercials) to research what's out there, what shows you might be auditioning for, what roles you might be right for, and what types you could play.

Also, a TV is good for your Comfort Zone. You will need an escape from time to time, a chance to relax and take your mind off your problems. There is no better way to lose yourself for a half an hour, or a couple hours then by tuning in to your favorite shows or a classic movie.

Take that occasional break, curl up on the couch, treat yourself to your favorite snack and do your..."research." If you're like most actors, a couple of hours spent watching other actors work on TV will inspire and motivate you to get back to your own acting.

8. Get a mentor. Another way to reinforce your Confidence is to find a mentor. A mentor is someone who believes in you as much as you believe in yourself...sometimes more.

This could be a manager, agent, casting director, acting coach or even a more experienced actor. Seek out someone whose life experiences have made them wise and compassionate, someone who might be busy in their own careers, but who can still give you quality time. He or she needs to be someone you can trust.

A mentor should be someone who's not competitive with you, but who understands your journey because they have either taken that journey or a similar one in their own life. They've seen what works and what doesn't. A mentor is someone who wants you to have a fulfilling life, someone who wants to help you fulfill your destiny.

Finding a mentor will take some time, especially in establishing a personal relationship. When you do find that mentor, be grateful and appreciative for that relationship, as well as for their insight and support.

I *am* a confident actor

It's important to remember that all the Talent in the world won't get you anywhere unless you have the Confidence in yourself and in your abilities. Talent and Confidence unite to mold you into a successful actor -- they rely on each other and actually strengthen each other.

Some of you (in fact, all of you at some point) will struggle to keep your Confidence growing. When it comes to maintaining your Confidence, you must always think of the reward -- a career as an actor. If that's your ultimate Want, then it's worth the struggle.

You must find the Confidence, believe in your Affirmations, work your craft, implement the successful habits of others, embrace who you are, and do what you need to do to get comfortable with your life as an actor in Hollywood. Once you have all of these elements clicking in high gear, you will find that you are more eager, more self-assured and most of all, more confident.

You know you have the Talent. You feel the Confidence. When you combine those two, you will be ready to face the most demanding of the Three Steps to Success...Perseverance.

CHAPTER 3
PERSEVERANCE

The third and final Step to Success is **Perseverance**.

As you're working your Talent and building your Confidence, you must now add Perseverance to this power pack in order to make it in Hollywood.

Perseverance is usually the most difficult step for actors to incorporate into their career because it requires an unshakable devotion to doing whatever it takes to accomplish your goals. Perseverance will test you more physically, emotionally and mentally than Talent and Confidence combined. It will test your endurance, your drive and your desire. It will test your *passion*.

In Hollywood, don't expect anybody to come knocking on your door and offer you a role. Don't expect anyone to call you out of the blue to offer you representation. Don't expect anyone to discover you at a club, mall or at the gym and offer you a three-picture deal.

Perseverance is about doing the *work* necessary to not only get noticed but also build a lasting career.

For the beginning actor, Perseverance is about doing the "grunt work," from getting headshots to doing agent mailings to signing up for casting websites, and so on.

For the more experienced actor, Perseverance is often more about longevity and staying in the game. Your Perseverance is what keeps you hanging in there, keeps you going, keeps you working at your craft and career in slow times and even slower times. Perseverance is what builds character.

Just like Talent and Confidence, we are all born with different levels of Perseverance. It is your instinctual Perseverance *combined* with your upbringing that has shaped your ability to endure.

Throughout this chapter, I'll help you define your own Perseverance and show you how vital it is to your career. I'll give you specific guidelines, tools and tasks for what you need to do to persevere. If you have the Want, the Talent and the Confidence behind you and if you're willing to commit to the Perseverance... you will succeed in fulfilling your dream.

What is Perseverance?

Perseverance is your tenacity, your resolve. You will be challenged many times in your acting career, from the moment you set foot in L.A. to the day you receive your Lifetime Achievement Award. Perseverance means staying the course, being strong, steadfast and even willing to make sacrifices to get your overall Want.

Think again of our Career Diet. If Talent is the protein and Confidence is the carbohydrates, then Perseverance would be your fruits and vegetables. You need all three for a healthy, well-balanced diet.

Perseverance gives you and your career the vitamins, minerals and nutrients it needs to survive. It's something that you need to do each and every day. Just like it's important to eat "an apple a day" or "finish your vegetables," you need to have your recommended daily allowance of Perseverance to round out your Career Diet.

What exactly does it mean to have Perseverance? It means that you are and always will be involved, active, BUSY, especially when it comes to your career. There are specific physical, mental and emotional traits that define someone who perseveres in their career.

Physically, Perseverance means:

• Waking up early to get a jump on your day.

• Working a minimum 40-hour work week.

• Setting daily, weekly and yearly goals and accomplishing them.

- Making strides to reach your career goals.
- Putting yourself out there...always.

Mentally, Perseverance means:

- Developing a natural curiosity and desire for the unknown.
- Having a willingness to learn and perfect.
- Saying "Yes" when everyone else is saying "No."
- Staying focused.
- Wanting more...always.

Emotionally, Perseverance means:

- To embrace any situation, any challenge.
- To stay calm and not let your emotions get in your way.
- Being willing to talk about how you're feeling.
- Acknowledging your frustrations and disappointments, and finding solutions.
- Staying patient...always.

All of these traits apply to an actor persevering in an acting career as well. The good news is that like Confidence, Perseverance is something that can be learned and as Yoda would say, "Learn you must." Like Talent, Perseverance is something that can be practiced (and yes, practice you must).

Before I teach you the ways and means to persevere, we need to once again determine how much Perseverance you came into this world with, how much you have now, and where you need to grow.

WHERE DOES PERSEVERANCE COME FROM?

Everybody has the ability to persevere. As with Talent and Confidence, we're all born with a certain amount of Perseverance in our genetic makeup. Even the least ambitious person on the planet has the ability and the instinct to persevere. Each and every one of us has the instinct to *survive.*

Our survival instincts include the need to eat, to drink, to breathe...to have sex! We all have the instincts that help us persevere to live. On top of these most raw, basic instincts, we also have hopes, dreams and desires.

Let's first see how much Perseverance you were born with and grew up with using our rating scale of 1 - 3 from the previous two chapters. Remember, this is to assess your natural ability to persevere. Again, if you have trouble recalling, ask your parents or whoever raised you.

Perseverance Scales:

The Instinctual Years (birth - five years old)

1 Rating: As a child, you didn't have the impetus or that early curiosity to walk and talk and so it took a little longer. You were content to play with whatever was given to you and to do what you were told, to stay in your Comfort Zone. You rarely asked "Why?"

2 Rating: You walked and talked at an early age. You were a little more curious. Your parents were constantly taking things away from you. You were the kid who climbed up on the counter to get the cookies, the kid who wondered what would happen if you put your peanut butter sandwich in the VCR. You enjoyed trying to figure things out on your own and working to accomplish a task. You often asked "Why?"

3 Rating: You were the prodigy. You showed signs of having a very strong will. You were infinitely curious about the world around you. You walked at a very early age. Once you started talking, you never stopped. You learned how to ask for and get what you wanted, and you were determined to get it, no matter what. You *always* asked "Why?" You were the "Why this? Why that? Why NOT?" kid.

Now that you've examined how much Perseverance you had when you came into this world, you must now once again look to see how it changed growing up.

The Formative Years (six years old - late teens)

1 Rating: As a child, and growing into your teen years, you may have been talented and smart and showed potential, but you weren't proactive. You needed to be pushed into activities. You didn't have the curiosity or motivation to be adventurous. You didn't feel the need to be ambitious. You might have had great ideas, but you never followed through. You rarely finished a project, never staying committed to something long enough to complete it.

2 Rating: You liked school and excelled throughout. You were very responsible. You often held jobs, whether it was a paper route, babysitting or flipping burgers at a fast food chain. You participated on a sports team, drama club, newspaper, etc. You knew how to balance everything you were doing. You worked hard and followed through at everything you did and you enjoyed the process.

3 Rating: At a young age, you had an extraordinary work ethic; you were always 110 percent committed to completing any task. Absolutely nothing would discourage you from achieving your goal. You started several programs, organized events, and managed projects. Everyone knew that you would be successful. Whether it was acting, playing the violin, singing, painting, you not only stuck to it, you mastered it. You may even have become professional or at least showed signs of achieving greatness later in life.

Once again, assess how you changed growing up. Did you move up or down from one scale to the next? Did you start out as a 2 and move up to a 3? Did you start as a 3 and move down a notch?

Just like Talent and Confidence, there are a number of factors that affect how much your ability to persevere changes throughout your life. Sure, it is up to each and every one of us to persevere in our own individual lives, no matter what our goals. How easy or difficult that is for us is determined initially by other influences, none more so than our upbringing.

Perseverance comes from your upbringing

You need to examine your upbringing, how you were raised, and how your Perseverance was either rewarded or ignored. Looking back to where you were as a child and young adult will help you understand what you need to do today to persevere.

Are you ACTOR A or ACTOR B?

ACTOR A: Did you have parents who taught you the importance of setting goals and encouraged your curiosity and drive? Were they there to see you through your school work, projects and activities? Did they set goals for you like getting good grades and insist that you accomplish them? Did they hold you accountable and reward you when you met your goals, whether it was a gold star, a trip to Disneyland or even money? Did they teach you the core values of responsibility and working hard to get what you want?

Or

ACTOR B: Did your parents, for whatever reason, not support you, push you or hold you accountable? Did they willingly or subconsciously discourage you from developing a solid work ethic? Did they neglect to teach you the value of staying focused or committed to completing a task or a project? When the task became difficult, were you told that you didn't have to finish? Were you sheltered and coddled or worse yet, were you left with no one to teach you how to persevere?

If you identify more with ACTOR A, chances are you have a clear understanding of what it is to persevere. You have the motivation to push through obstacles and accomplish your goals. You were rewarded for not just achieving goals, but also for the pursuit of those goals. That motivation, support and discipline has probably carried over to your life today, giving you a strong work ethic.

If you fall more under ACTOR B, you're less likely to understand what it will take for you to persevere. It doesn't mean you can't persevere, it just means that the process might be more unfamiliar and thus, a bit more challenging.

Perseverance ALSO comes from...

• **Ancestry:** We've talked about how our Perseverance comes from our genes, which we inherit from our parents, our grandparents, our ancestors. If you're able to, look deeper into your family history. If you come from ancestors who are part of a disenfranchised group that dealt with oppression, repression or persecution, then you might be part of a bloodline that *inherently* knows how to persevere.

Families who have risen above great struggles to become successful are the epitome of self-sacrifice, determination, hard work and Perseverance.

What have *your* ancestors endured? What lessons have you learned from stories of the "old days," listening to grandma and grandpa talk of struggles in their life? How has their Perseverance, their tenacity shaped and influenced your life?

• **Instinctual curiosity:** Some of us are just simply born more curious than others. Not only is it instinctual, it's intellectual. There is something in our brain that makes us want to learn more about the world around us, to educate ourselves so we can ultimately be more in control of our destinies.

Our curiosity not only propels us to inquire, investigate and study, it also *motivates* us. We want to know what else is out there, we want to know if we can do better. From childhood on, there are those of us who are not content to simply settle for what we're told; we want to know the reason why. "Why?" is as important of a question as "How?" to somebody who has Perseverance. That perpetual curiosity is at the core of people who persevere.

• **Competitive spirit:** Some people are born naturally more competitive than others. Again, think of Tiger Woods. Sure, he was born with a tremendous amount of Talent and Confidence and had the support of his family. But there was something else that made him great, something else that pushed him to be the best.

Tiger Woods, Donald Trump, Dick Clark, Sean "Puffy" Combs, Steven Spielberg, Martha Stewart, Oprah Winfrey, Ryan Seacrest, Madonna, anyone who has made it to the pinnacle of their career, is born with a competitive spirit. These people are not content with second place. They want to be the best at what they do…and not just the best today, but the best *ever*. More importantly, they're willing to do the work required to be the best because that's how you win!

YOU CAN PERSEVERE

Perseverance is something that can be learned, studied and implemented. Just like Confidence, no matter how little or how much overall Perseverance you were born with or have now, you will need to learn a whole new kind of Perseverance…an **Acting Perseverance**. It is this Acting Perseverance that will directly relate to your career, to the work you will have to do to reach your *acting* goals.

Throughout the rest of this chapter, I'll give you some very specific tasks you can (and need to) do to persevere in your acting career.

First things first, let's mentally prepare you.

Exercise: I persevered when I...

Before I give you specific Perseverance tasks, I need to show you that you are capable of persevering; that you're ready to take on this demanding Step to Success.

I want you to think about something of importance that you persevered at in the past, something you willed yourself to do, a specific goal you've accomplished in your life. Keep it away from acting. It can be winning an award, making a sports team, learning to play an instrument, finishing a writing project, running a marathon, completing college, quitting smoking, etc.

Whatever it is, I want you to write it down in your Actor's Journal:

"I persevered when I_____."

I want you to closely examine what you've written down and think of what you did to accomplish that specific goal. What steps did you take physically, mentally and emotionally in the pursuit of that goal? What exactly did you do, from planning to execution and everything in between?

Take a few minutes to write down 10 things in your Actor's Journal that you did to achieve that goal. It will probably be easy for you to think of the physical steps you took, but challenge yourself to think of the mental and emotional steps you had to take.

"In order to accomplish my goal, I..."

For example, here's what Jeff, a student of mine, wrote down when he did this exercise in my class.

EXAMPLE:

I persevered when I...won my college essay award.

In order to accomplish my goal, I...

1. Took as many writing classes as I could.
2. Set daily goals for writing the essay.
3. Sat my butt down to work on my essay at least an hour a day for a month.
4. Spent hours researching the topic I was writing about.
5. Got lots of critique from friends and professors.
6. Edited my essay five times!
7. Got less sleep, watched less football (bummer).
8. Sacrificed time hanging out with my friends and girlfriend (major bummer).
9. Borrowed $100 from my parents to submit for the award.
10. Rewarded myself after each accomplishment (beer and Cheetos).

How does Jeff's list compare to yours?

Once you've completed your list, you can see the sacrifices you've made and the commitment it took to persevere at your specific goal. Let this list be a reminder that you have the power to not only *set* a goal, but to *complete* that goal.

As you begin to work on your Acting Perseverance, you must always remember that you have persevered before and you can persevere now.

Actually, you'll find that persevering in an acting career is not that different from persevering in anything else you want to accomplish.

Look over your list and check how many of these could apply to your acting career. If you wrote down that you had to set daily goals, you know you have to set daily *acting career* goals. If you wrote down that you had to practice a lot...then you know you have to practice *acting* a lot. If you wrote down you had to sacrifice hanging out with your friends...you get where I'm going.

In order to be successful in any career, you need to first have a goal and then a plan. The same is true when it comes to your acting career. That is what Perseverance is all about. If you want to persevere in an acting career, you have to know...

THE FOUR P's OF PERSEVERANCE
Purpose
Pursuit
Patience
Persistence

Perseverance is having *Persistence* and *Patience* in the *Pursuit* of your *Purpose*.

Make this your Perseverance mantra. Write it down in your Actor's Journal. It will define all the "work" you need to do to build your career as an actor, especially when you're first getting started.

You need Persistence and Patience in the Pursuit of your acting career to reach your Purpose of being a successful actor.

This Perseverance formula applies to everything from accomplishing simple every day career tasks to achieving lifelong career goals.

Purpose

You need to know what you Want, what you're fighting for, what you're trying to accomplish. It's your goal, your mission, your **Purpose**.

If you know what you Want, then you already know...your Purpose is to be a successful actor.

You want to fulfill your destiny, to bring great light, energy, compassion, happiness and love into the world through your art. You want to entertain, inspire, enlighten, touch and move others. Your Purpose is to act.

You need to know your Purpose and constantly put it out there for the universe to hear.

Pursuit

Pursuit is about having a plan. Pursuit is defining exactly what you need to do to accomplish your goal (your Purpose). It's drawing a blueprint, setting the roadmap, making the plans to stay on course.

For actors, there really isn't a set plan. It's not like being a doctor, an accountant, a lawyer or an engineer, where there is mandatory schooling, followed by internships, jobs and then a career. In the acting business, the only thing that actors share is a Want, a desire, a need to act.

While you will receive a lot of advice on how to approach your career, the details and the execution of any plan really depend on you and your individual goals. How you choose to go about working at those individual goals is how you define your Pursuit.

If you want to see an up close, personal and funny example of an actor's Pursuit, watch stand up comedian Kathy Griffin. Although she's had success in television and film, she hasn't yet reached her goal to be on Hollywood's A-List. She's turned her constant struggle into the hit reality show *My Life on the D-List,* where she showcases the trials and tribulations of her career in Hollywood. Her show gives a glimpse of just how diligently a performer has to work on their career every single day. Kathy Griffin knows what she wants, has a plan, works hard, and often struggles in her Pursuit.

Patience

This is about all the *mental* and *emotional* work required to achieve your goal. It's accepting what you need to do to fulfill your Purpose. It's preparing yourself for the fact that fulfilling your Purpose might not be quick or easy. It's being willing to stay calm and focused on the task at hand no matter what obstacles get in your way. It's about having **Patience**.

It's the "hurry up and wait" mentality.

"Hurry up and wait" is a familiar phrase for many different artists in L.A. I believe it originated on movie sets. Actors would hurry on to the set to do a take, only to have to "wait" for the crew to get everything prepped. When that happens to an actor, they need to stay in character, stay focused on the scene.

This translates to your acting career as well. The phrase "hurry up and wait" means landing a meeting with an agent only to wait for his or her phone call, rushing to an audition only to wait for your name to be called, getting a callback only to wait to hear if you got the job.

The "wait" is about having Patience.

It's about concentrating on your tasks, keeping yourself motivated, and not letting your emotions get the best of you. Having Patience will help you stay in the game through successful times and slow times. You need to be patient before you get your big break, in between your big break and your next job, and so on. What you're doing during the time you're waiting is often most important. It's about working hard and being ready for your opportunities. It's about always having...

Persistence

Persistence is the heart and soul of Perseverance. This means doing all the work, taking the *physical* steps necessary to follow through with your Pursuit. Being constantly persistent in your Pursuit will fulfill your Purpose.

Every actor trying to make it in Hollywood has to go through a process to establish themselves, to start their acting career. This process will consist of doing a lot of "grunt work."

What I mean by grunt work is getting headshots, writing a resume, researching agents and managers, doing mailings, signing up for casting websites, and so on. It's all the work that will help you build a *career* while you learn your *craft*. Grunt work is the foundation of Perseverance.

Being persistent in this grunt work will get your foot in the door and produce positive results. It's your Persistence that will keep you going no matter what. Staying persistent will establish that solid foundation, a strong work ethic that will carry you throughout your career.

Your Perseverance starts now!

The next part of this chapter will be your Perseverance "To-Do" list. I will give you some specific tasks and guidelines you must accomplish to get your career up and running. As you approach this Perseverance work, always remember your Four P's.

Some of you may be starting at the beginning and this will lay out your first priorities. For those of you who have done some of this work, let this serve as a reminder or even a fresh approach.

Also, be aware that everybody in this town has a different opinion of how to handle some of this career work. The trick is to be open-minded and willing to try different strategies until you find the one that works best for you.

With that said…welcome to the *School of Perseverance.*

In this school, you will learn the importance of always having a plan and a strong work ethic. You will learn that an acting career is a process. You will learn how to stay patient and positive and feeling like you're making progress, whether you're just starting out or if you've been in the game for years.

Before you begin your School of Perseverance, you need to get settled and get into acting class. In the first two chapters, I emphasized the importance of establishing yourself in Los Angeles, building up a Comfort Zone, and working on your Talent and Confidence. You need to have your life in order before you can think of tackling your career. Most important, you need to be a trained actor.

Let's assume you're settled into Los Angeles and you're studying your craft. You're then ready to move on to the next phase of your career, the bulk of your Perseverance work. Your career in Hollywood is really about two specific tasks, two necessities vital to any acting career:

1. Getting representation.
2. Getting acting work.

These are your first two priorities. Once you accomplish them, you will begin to see an acting career unfold before your very eyes.

PRIORITY #1: GET REPRESENTATION

What I mean by representation is an agent or manager, a professional in the industry who will help guide you on your career path and get you acting opportunities.

There are many different ways to go about getting an agent or manager. For some of you, this process *will* take time, but finding an agent or manager is of the utmost importance. An agent or manager will know how to market you. They have the relationships with casting directors, which means they have the ability to get you auditions. Good representation will advise you and help you manage your career.

How can you get an agent or manager to notice you?

First, you need to put together a **Pitch Package**. A Pitch Package will provide agents and managers with a clear idea of your look, personality, training and experience. The three necessities you need to have in your Pitch Package are:

Headshots
Resume
Monologues

Headshots

Your **headshots** are your calling cards. They are very important because they will be the first (and often the only) piece of self-marketing that agents, managers and even casting directors will see. You need to have a headshot that shows you at your best, one that captures your personality.

Your headshot needs to be taken by a professional L.A or New York photographer. There is a specific style, look and feel to these headshots. BUT, you should not spend a lot of money on your *first round* of headshots in Los Angeles. Time and time again, I hear stories of actors who drop hundreds of dollars on their first headshots only to have an agent request that they get new ones once they get signed.

The purpose of this first round of headshots is to simply get noticed by an agent or manager. Find an inexpensive yet respectable photographer, talk to him or her, and make sure you'd be comfortable shooting with them. Feeling comfortable with your headshot photographer will help you relax and bring out your true personality.

What kind of headshots should you get? Well, it helps if you at least have a sense of your type and how you might be marketable (refer back to The Typing Game). If you're the "cute but goofy best friend" type, don't get headshots that portray you as the leading man. There are many actors that think they're the ingénues or leading men when they are really character actors (and could get a lot more work as such).

Make sure you have both a commercial and theatrical picture, both measuring 8x10. In simpler terms, have one of you smiling and one more serious. There are several different styles for these pictures, be it close-up or three-quarter (which are industry terms for how much of your face and body the headshot shows). With trends in headshots constantly changing, make sure to research what kind of headshots are popular now. As a general note, you can't go wrong with a color headshot that clearly shows your face.

Since most photographers shoot digitally these days, you will take hundreds of pictures in your session. You should have no problem finding both a commercial and theatrical headshot you can use. When choosing your headshots, you should seek out the advice of others in the industry. When it comes right down to it, though, you ultimately need to trust your own instincts. You need to have a photo that you're proud of, one that excites you.

Go to a reproduction house (reputable ones in L.A. are Reproductions, Argentum Photo Lab and Isgo Lepejian Custom Photo Lab) and get around 500 professional copies of your chosen shots.

You should also get postcards (typically 5.5x3.5) of your smiling look (commercial) and your serious look (theatrical). These postcards will be used for following up after your first agent/manager mailing (more on that later). Also, get yourself a standard-size business card featuring your headshot and contact info that you can hand out at networking events. In Los Angeles, there are a number of printing shops that will offer deals on mass quantities of business cards.

Once you have your headshots, postcards and business cards printed, it's time to add the resume.

Resume

On the back of your headshot, you need to have a **resume** that shows the potential agent or manager what you've done and what you are currently doing.

If you can, print your resume right on the back of your 8x10 headshots as it looks cleaner and more professional. If you can't, simply trim your resume so it fits the borders of your headshot and staple it on the back. Also, keep it neat! Make sure everything is spelled right, aligned properly...and there are no coffee ring stains on it.

More important is what's *in* your resume. First and foremost, you need to have all of your contact information, including your cell phone number, e-mail address and website if you have one. You should list your height, weight and even eye and hair color. However, never list your age as it could limit the roles you get called in for.

Then, put any and all acting experience you have, be it theatre (college, community, professional), independent films, commercial work, music videos, industrials, etc. Be honest. Don't lie. Don't "pad" your resume.

Make sure you highlight what acting teachers or studios you have studied with or who you are currently studying with. Agents and managers put great value on actors that are studying with L.A. teachers.

Finally, make sure to include a short list of special skills, whether it be singing, dancing, accents, sports, music, rock climbing, fencing, juggling, cooking, poker, animal noises, etc. The more specific, the better. Please note...save yourself, your agent and the casting director a lot of time by being honest and proficient in the special skills you list.

Monologues

Obviously, a **monologue** isn't something you physically include in your Pitch Package, but it's something you need to have ready at a moment's notice. There will be times when you'll hit it off with an agent in a meeting and they'll want to see your acting capabilities right there and then. They'll ask you to do a monologue on the spot and you'll need to have one in your back pocket, ready to go.

I recommend having *two* different kinds of monologues at your disposal: one comedic and one dramatic. These monologues should be no longer than two minutes and they should showcase your best acting strengths and characters that you would likely play.

So if you're 21 years old, don't do Willy Loman from *Death of a Salesman*. If you're 40 years old, don't do Laura from *The Glass Menagerie*. When meeting an agent or manager, find a monologue that suits your age and type, one that you can naturally and organically identify with, a role that you can be cast in.

You can get monologues from monologue books as well as several different websites. Make sure you browse until you find the best one for you. Also, feel free to use pieces from TV and film, though I would recommend against performing a famous scene. It's always good to find monologues that these agents and managers haven't seen time and time again.

Now that you have your headshots, postcards, business cards and resumes all ready to go and two monologues at your disposal, you are ready to do your agent/manager mailing and hopefully get a meeting. I have a two-part process to these mailings:

The First Agent/Manager Mailing

Your first agent/manager mailing really serves two purposes. One, it will introduce you to the acting community, giving industry professionals their first glance at the new kid in town. Two, it will hopefully land you an agent or manager.

When you actually do your first mailing depends upon your experience and training. You should have a year or so of training and intense study behind you before you seek representation. That's the minimum! Remember, you need to be ready and prepared when you start getting sent out on auditions. If you've been taking classes regularly, graduated from a four-year program, trained in New York, London or Chicago, or have some previous acting experience, then you are ready to send out your headshots.

You need to get a book of agency and manager listings, which can be found at any of the local acting book shops (the most popular is Samuel French Theatre and Film Book Shop, which has locations in Hollywood and the Valley). There are several different agency and manager books to choose from, and they are updated every month. They provide all the essential information you need to do a mailing, from contact information to what types these agents and managers are currently seeking.

For this first mailing, my advice is to send out your pictures to as many agents and managers as possible (at least a 100) along with a short, simple cover letter explaining who you are and stating that you're seeking representation.

EXAMPLE:

Dear Agent or Manager,

Hi, my name is Ben Smith and I am currently seeking representation. I have been studying on-camera acting with Scott Sedita Acting Studios for the past year and I am eager to begin auditioning. I have heard wonderful things about your agency and would love the opportunity to meet with you. Enclosed is my headshot and resume. Please feel free to call or e-mail me anytime. Thank you for your time and consideration. I hope to hear from you soon.

Sincerely, Ben Smith

Consider your first mailing a positive spin on the "throw it out there and see what sticks" philosophy. In my experience, it works. Not only does it improve your odds of actually getting a meeting with an agent or manager, it's also a declaration of sorts to yourself, the industry and the universe that you're ready to start your career. It's almost like an official announcement that your acting career is open for business.

These mailings involve a lot of the tedious grunt work. You will need to research each agency or management firm, personalize each cover letter, type out the labels, get stamps, make several trips to the post office, and so on. If you send out 100 headshots, you might only get a few phone calls and maybe (if you're lucky) one or two meetings. You might get nothing at all.

Truthfully, that's not what's important right now. What you're trying to accomplish is to get yourself in the habit of doing this kind of grunt work and building a strong work ethic. Consider this your *practice* mailing. Hopefully it will pay off. Even if it doesn't, your second and future mailings will be easier because now you understand everything involved in the process.

Two weeks after your first agent or manager mailing, follow it up by sending a postcard to everyone on your list.

EXAMPLE:

Hello,

I just wanted to follow up to make sure you received my headshot and resume. I hope to hear from you and have the opportunity to meet with you about possible representation.

Thanks, Ben Smith

The Second Agent/Manager Mailing

After your first headshot and postcard mailing, you will (you should) find yourself getting more educated about your acting career. You will learn a lot more about the business, be it from other actors, in acting class, your own research, reading trade publications like *Backstage West, The Hollywood Reporter* and *Variety.* One of the things you will hear and read a lot about are various agents and managers.

You'll learn what agents and managers your friends and classmates have, what new agencies and management firms are opening up, who's currently seeking actors, what types they're looking for, etc.

Plus, you will learn more about *yourself.* As you continue your training, you will begin to see more and more what types you can play and how you can market yourself in Hollywood.

Within a year of your initial mailing, you will take all that you've learned about yourself and the business and do your second agent and manager mailing. This one will be a little more focused.

Prep your headshots (whether they're the same ones or new ones), update your resume, and include an even more detailed cover letter. Don't just introduce yourself, give some details about your type, your potential niche and how you see yourself as an actor.

EXAMPLE:

Dear Agent or Manager,

Hi, my name is Ben Smith and I am currently seeking representation. I have been studying on-camera acting with Scott Sedita Acting Studios for the past year and a half and I am eager to begin auditioning. I am a young Zach Braff type, a lovable loser with a Midwestern innocence who has enough depth to play drama, but whose strength lies in his biting, sometimes sarcastic comedic timing.

I have heard wonderful things about your agency and would love the opportunity to meet with you. Enclosed is my headshot and resume. Please feel free to call or e-mail me anytime. Thank you for your time and consideration. I hope to hear from you soon.

Sincerely, Ben Smith

If you can, it's always good to have a "referred by" in your cover letter. If you heard about the agent or manager from someone, ask if you can mention their name.

This time around, you are only sending your Pitch Package to those agents or managers that might be looking for your type. I would say that you should send it out to your top 25 agencies. Be sure to look for agencies that could actually work with you in building your career and helping you get career opportunities. Too many actors want to jump to major firms like ICM or William Morris when they would be better suited working with a mid-sized firm or even a boutique agency that would make them a priority.

Once again, two weeks later, follow up with a postcard. Since this is your second round and the mailing is more focused, your chances of getting an agent or manager should increase.

After your second mailing, the only other time you will send out your headshots or postcards will be when you have something to report, like you're working on a TV show, film, play, showcase, you name it. Make sure you send out these announcements as it will impress agents and managers to see that you are an actor that works.

When I worked as an agent, I had an actor who seemed to send me a postcard every month, updating me as to what he was doing, whether it was a showcase, an industrial or an Off-Off Broadway play. His name was Michael. When I finally met him, his headshot reflected his look and his personality. He was an intense and charismatic young actor with a good sense of humor. He knew who he was and what type he played best. He had an ethnic New

York look with a nice, big nose that he wasn't afraid to show off. I was impressed with him, his training and his Perseverance.

Unfortunately, I had a client just like Michael so I couldn't sign him. The good thing was that he was just as persistent with other agents in New York as he was with me. Soon after meeting with me, Michael got an agent. Later, I heard he was working and doing some great stage work in New York. Then one day I turned on HBO to watch a new show called *The Sopranos* and I saw Michael in a perfect role as Tony Soprano's nephew Christopher Moltisanti. The Michael who sent me all those postcards was Michael Imperioli.

Adding To Your Pitch Package

There are some things that you can do that can impress, boost your chances, and raise your stock value in the eyes of an agent or manager. Along with having extensive acting training, adding a demo reel and having union membership can make your Pitch Package look all the more impressive.

• **Demo Reels:** Seeing you on tape interacting, reacting and acting will give an agent a better sense of who you are, the parts you're right for and what you're capable of. In fact, more and more agents are requesting to see some footage when they meet with new actors.

A demo reel is a walking, talking headshot. It's a short (and I emphasize *short*) collection of your best work, highlighting your acting capabilities. A demo reel can consist of footage from independent films, student films, self-produced projects and sometimes even recorded class work. There are several different schools of thought for how these demo reels should be produced. As a general rule, they should be two to three minutes long, involving your best scene or two and possibly a short montage of you in various roles.

You need to make sure that when you're acting in a project that you always get your footage. BUT, it's important that your demo reel include only *high quality* footage...and that's where most actors run into problems. For many of you, the footage you have of yourself is probably poor quality (or worse). Sending in an unprofessional or sloppy demo reel is detrimental to your cause. However, if you have some good footage that shows off your acting chops and is professionally filmed on high quality digital video, it can be a powerful accessory.

• **SAG Card/AFTRA membership:** One of your overall goals when getting to Hollywood will be to eventually join the Screen Actors Guild (SAG) and/or the American Federation of Television and Radio Artists (AFTRA), the two major unions for actors around the country.

The rules, as well as the cost involved, in joining these two unions seem to be ever-changing. Keep yourself up to date by checking out **sag.org** and **aftra.com** and reading the industry trades.

Getting your union card is an important step for any actor in Hollywood. It's a rite of passage that signifies that you're now part of the same fraternity of professional actors.

Before you join SAG or AFTRA, you should do as much non-union work as you can to build up your resume. When you book your first SAG job, you are then SAG-eligible. You can continue to do nonunion work until you book another union job and become a "must-join." Once you have joined SAG or AFTRA, you are then essentially barred from doing nonunion work. So make sure you only join when you are ready to make that leap.

Being a union actor or even SAG-eligible looks impressive on your resume. You know what else looks good? Working in the business! When you've got an agent or you're at least in the process of getting an agent, you're ready to move on to your next Perseverance Priority.

PRIORITY #2: GET ACTING WORK

You don't have to sit back and wait for an agent to get you acting jobs in Hollywood. In fact, you can't. You need to work hard to fill your resume. Sure, you will work closely with your agent and manager and do everything you can to help them market you. After all, they are the ones that are going to get you your bigger acting opportunities...when you're ready. There is a lot of acting work that you can get on your own to not only kick start, but also maintain your acting career.

Theatre

Who says that theatre only lives in New York? As I mentioned in the Talent chapter, Los Angeles has a vibrant theatre community, ranging from nationally recognizable playhouses like the Geffen Playhouse and the Mark Taper Forum to hundreds of small theatre troupes.

Joining a theatre company is a great way to keep yourself consistently working at your craft. Granted, it's no substitute for class, but performing with a theatre company keeps your acting skills sharp. Theatre also provides a great place for you to be seen, to network, and to meet other actors, producers, directors and writers.

Theatre companies epitomize Perseverance. Working at a theatre company typically involves a lot more work than simply acting. Actors help put up the shows, whether it's stage managing, building sets, lighting, sound design, marketing, promoting the show, working the box office, and even writing, directing and producing. It's a great way to keep you busy, keep you involved, and give you the full theatrical experience from start to finish.

Backstage West provides an annual listing of legitimate theatre companies in Los Angeles. You should expect to pay some minimal dues to be part of any theatre company. While this might not be the norm elsewhere, most local theatre troupes charge company dues, typically around $30 to $50 a month.

Showcases

Showcases are an opportunity for an actor to "showcase" their Talent for industry guests; including agents, managers and casting directors.

These showcases are run by industry professionals and feature actors working on short, individual scenes or monologues, typically in a theatre space or an acting studio.

There is usually a charge for participating in a showcase, sometimes in the hundreds of dollars. Before signing on, I strongly suggest getting a recommendation from an actor who's worked with the director running the showcase. Unfortunately, there are a number of showcases that do not pull in an industry audience and you don't want to waste your time or money.

Actor showcases are a great opportunity for you to work weeks and even months on a scene. Along with having that tremendous acting experience, the main point of these showcases is to highlight your acting abilities and get seen by the industry. As an agent and casting director, I found many actors from showcases. But be warned, you should only do a showcase when you are *ready* to "showcase" your acting.

Student Films/Independent Films

Every week, you can open up a *Backstage West*, look at the casting notices and see dozens of non-union, small independent and student films that are looking for actors. You can also check casting notices on websites like ActorsAccess and NowCasting (more on those later).

For those actors ready to audition, submit yourself for as many of these projects as possible. Remember that part of Perseverance is constantly putting yourself out there. Think of these auditions as your rehearsal, a great opportunity to practice for when you have to audition for professional casting directors.

For the most part, these independent film directors and writers are inexperienced as well, so the playing field is leveled. You don't have to feel intimidated by them or the process. This is your training ground for not only learning how to audition, but also for working on an actual set (however minimal) and collaborating with directors and writers.

It's also a great way to get your name and face out there. If you do good work, you will get recommendations and other opportunities. I had one student who did a USC film and the director liked her Talent, personality and work ethic so much that he told several other directors about her. She ended up doing three more USC projects within a couple months.

If you submit for these projects, you WILL get called in to audition and you WILL book. Not only is that exciting (and often a much-needed Confidence booster) it can also potentially lead to great footage for your demo reel and to making strong contacts. Remember, this town is filled with up-and-coming directors as well.

With a handful of film schools around Hollywood, like USC and UCLA, and hundreds of aspiring filmmakers, there are plenty of acting opportunities. Who knows? Maybe you'll work with the next George Lucas or Steven Spielberg...both USC grads.

Producing Your Own Projects

Actually, you don't have to wait to be cast in a USC, UCLA or independent film project. You can star in, write, direct or produce your own. And why not? With technological advances in digital cameras, anybody can be a budding filmmaker. Plus, with the enormous popularity of websites like YouTube, MySpace and Facebook, there are now outlets and opportunities for thousands of people to check out these amateur works.

It's important to *self-produce*. These projects will keep you working, keep you out there, and potentially open up some doors.

These days, self-producing is one of the best ways to get noticed quickly in Hollywood. Writing and producing your own work will keep you working on your craft and put you on the fast-track to building your career. You can write, produce and/or direct your own project, whether it's a monologue, sketch or even a short or feature length film. If done well, these projects can go a lot further than a headshot or demo reel when trying to attract industry attention.

Sometimes these self-produced projects can even capture *national* attention. Think of Andy Samberg. He self-produced a number of shorts that attracted the attention of *Saturday Night Live*...which signed him on as a cast member!

With all the other struggling actors, writers and directors in Hollywood, you have the opportunity to jumpstart your career by forming your own mini-independent production company and putting together your own projects. And you should! I'm not talking about a multi-million dollar corporation. I'm suggesting a few dollars, a good camera, a handful of creative ideas and a group of equally ambitious people.

Having something in your hand that you've completed on your own can only help you. It's a great lesson in Perseverance. It's a lot of hard work, time, energy and even money, but the payoff will be worth it.

That being said, your best bet to getting acting work in Hollywood is to...

Help Your Agent Or Manager

Okay, you've done everything you need to do: you got your headshots, resume, a demo reel and even your SAG card. You've done several independent films, you're part of a theatre company, and you've even produced your own short video that you put up on YouTube. Because of your Perseverance, all your hard work, blood, sweat and tears...you've got an agent!

So now you can sit back, let your agent field offers and wait for the auditions to roll in, right?

Wrong!

Just because you have representation, your Perseverance work doesn't stop. You have to put yourself in the mindframe that all your agent or manager really is at this point is a letterhead. Yes, having representation is a gateway to opening up career opportunities, but you need to be diligent in doing whatever you can to help your agent or manager market and sell you.

When you sign with an agent or manager, you not only enter into a legally binding contract, you also enter into a mutual *partnership*. For your representation, they agree to develop, groom, market and advise you on your career, as well as get you out on auditions. For you, it means listening to the advice of your agent or manager, keeping your acting training active, getting coaching for auditions, continuing to get work on your own and doing anything and everything that can help this "team" make you a success.

Don't just talk about doing things to help your representation... do them! Have your headshots with you at all times, check your voice mail and e-mail regularly, have your Actor's Journal handy to write down appointments, and confirm appointments immediately. Make sure you're prepared for any and all auditions, and most importantly, listen to your agent or manager's advice.

You need to inspire and excite your agent or manager, reassure them that you're ready to work with them, whether it's getting new headshots, formulating a plan, setting goals or whatever else needs to be done. Show them that you're a professional, ambitious, collaborative, hard-working actor that's willing to persevere and is worth representing and sending out.

On top of that, there are some specific things you can do to help your representation get you acting work:

- Sign up for acting websites
- Do casting director mailings
- Attend casting director workshops
- Research
- Network
- Be prepared for audition

• **Sign up for acting websites:** There are several reputable acting websites that list audition notices and give actors a chance to post pictures, resumes, video clips and a profile for directors and casting directors to peruse. You should be signed up and keep updating these sites as often as possible. The top sites are:

ActorsAccess.com
NowCasting.com
LAcasting.com

There are several others, but these are the three you need to have bookmarked. Submit yourself for casting notices on these sites and you'll probably be called in to audition here and there. It's important to note that you should check with your representation to make sure they're okay with you submitting on your own. If you do get called in from your own submission, inform your agent or manager immediately.

You can also set up your own website with pictures and information on your acting career, a blog, etc. Or take advantage of community sites like MySpace or Facebook to set up a profile and even include photos and clips of your work.

• **Do casting director mailings:** You can handle this much the same way you did your agent/manager mailing. First of all, make sure you're trained and ready to audition. Then send out a mass mailing to both commercial and theatrical casting directors with your headshot and resume, now with your agent or manager information, letting them know you are available for castings. Remember, the point, once again, is to announce yourself, this time to the casting world.

Your chances of getting a response on a blind mailing are slim, but I do know of some actors who have gotten called in for auditions from such mailings, especially commercially.

A few months after this mass mailing, you will do another casting director mailing, this one a little more focused. Find the casting directors that cast TV shows that might use your type or those that are currently casting feature films. Keep your agent or manager informed of any auditions you get.

• **Attend casting director workshops:** These workshops are not only a great way to nurture your Talent, they are also a way to get some face time with casting directors or their associates. Sometimes your agent or manager will recommend that you take a casting director workshop in order for you to meet a specific casting director.

These workshops typically charge a fee and feature a casting director discussing the business and then maybe critiquing some scene work from the actors. There are groups that you can join (Actorsite, The Actor's Network and Industry RSVP) that offer discounts for these workshops. If you have some extra cash, they are a great way to meet casting directors.

• **Research:** I know the word "research" conjures up memories of late nights at the library or online, running through textbooks, articles and speeches, prepping for that dreaded final paper. Don't panic, I'm not asking for a dissertation. I'm just telling you to keep your eyes and ears open for information that pertains to your career. You need to be knowledgeable about your business.

If you really want to help your agent or manager, learn the game. You need to keep on top on what's happening in this business, especially anything that could potentially affect you and your acting career.

One of the best ways to research is to watch TV and go to the movies.

As I've laid out in the Talent and Confidence chapters, watching TV (including commercials) will help you gain a general knowledge of what's happening in the industry, what TV genres are hot now, what types of shows you're right for, and what types of roles you'd be cast in.

Watching TV will also help you with your auditions. There are many different genres of TV shows, and it is your responsibility to understand the type of genre you are auditioning for. You have to know the *tone* of the show you're going in for and you can really only learn that by watching the show itself. You don't have to watch every single episode, but enough for you to get a feeling for the show as a whole. Here are the most common genres with some TV show examples (new and old):

SHOW GENRES:

- **Single-camera comedy** (*Sex and the City, The Office, Entourage, Curb Your Enthusiasm*)
- **Multi-camera comedy** (*Friends, Will & Grace, Two and a Half Men, The New Adventures of Old Christine*)
- **Sketch comedy** (*Saturday Night Live, Mad TV*)
- **Dramedy** (*Desperate Housewives, Ugly Betty, Boston Legal*)
- **Drama** (*The Sopranos, 24, Lost, Heroes, Brothers & Sisters*)
- **Medical drama** (*ER, Grey's Anatomy, House M.D.*)
- **Procedural drama** (*CSI, Law & Order, Without a Trace*)
- **Soap operas** (*General Hospital, All My Children, One Life to Live*)

Within these genres, each individual show has its own tone. The tone of *Entourage* is very different from *The Office*. The tone of *CSI* is very different from *Law and Order* (I'd say that the tone of each *CSI* and *Law & Order* series is actually different from each other). While good acting is good acting, you will need to know the tone of each particular show and adjust your work accordingly.

Of course, research goes beyond just watching TV or going to the movies. You need to keep up on the industry buzz. You need to read the trade publications and the local newspapers, regularly check the acting websites, stay current on basic SAG and AFTRA rules and regulations, talk to your acting coach, other actors, your colleagues, peers, etc.

Make sure you keep a record of everything in your Actor's Journal. This is your ultimate collection of information to help you with your career. Each time you jot something down, make sure to date the page for easy reference. Remember, the more of these notebooks you fill, the busier you are as an actor.

Read, talk, watch and listen. The more informed you are, the more prepared you can be as you persevere.

• **Network:** Though networking is a challenge for many actors, you need to learn how to do it. Many opportunities come from networking, and you have to get comfortable with the process. You will find yourself at parties and industry functions talking to casting directors, writers, directors, producers, etc. You need to know how to approach them.

For those of you terrified of the thought, here's a real simple approach for you to take at your next industry function if you see a casting director you'd like to meet:

First, take a deep breath and put a self-assured smile on your face. Approach the casting director with Confidence and make sure you wait for the right opportunity -- do not interrupt them if they're in the middle of a conversation. When you see your chance, make eye contact and simply say something like the following:

*"Hi, I'm Ben Smith and I just wanted to tell you that I love
the casting you did on your last film (or current TV show),
and I hope to someday audition for you."*

Hopefully, that casting director will say "Thank you." That's where
you should expect the conversation to end. If the casting director
does strike up a conversation with you -- asking you who you are,
where you studied, what work you've done -- make sure you have
a short, prepared answer. You should be friendly, charming and
open...not needy. Having a good sense of humor always works,
too. Most important, though, be yourself! When the conversation
dies down, say, "It was nice to meet you," and move on. Hopefully
you'll walk away with their business card. If they do offer you a
card, be sure to hand them one of your headshot business cards in
return.

• **Be prepared for auditions:** There is nothing as important to
your representation than you being prepared *for* your auditions
and being professional *in* your auditions.

Here are some tips to help you do your best at any audition:

• Be prepared and do all of your homework. That means breaking
  down the script. WOFAIM it and memorize it as best you can
  (if you've worked on your sides long enough, you'll naturally
  memorize it).

• Leave your homework at home.

• Dress like the character would dress, but don't ever wear a
  costume.

• BE ON TIME!

• Don't "chat up the waiting room." Use this time to prepare --
  mentally, emotionally and physically -- for your audition rather
  than chatting with the other actors. Don't psyche yourself out
  and don't let others psyche you out either. Stay focused.

- Walk in to the casting room with a good attitude, not desperate to get the job.

- Be friendly and charming with the people in the room, but don't talk too much. A nervous actor will talk too much and end up with his foot in his mouth.

- Your script is your best friend. Be off book, but hold it in your hand. Don't rumple it, roll it up or shove it in your back pocket.

- Make eye contact with your reader, but don't stare them down.

- Be confident and have fun. Know that this is your time -- you were asked to audition and you've earned the right to be there. So enjoy it; if you're having fun, the casting director will have fun.

- If you feel like you're off to a bad start, politely ask the casting director if you can start again. They will most likely say yes. However, if you're midway through the audition, refocus and finish the job.

- After your audition, you can sometimes ask (if it feels right), "Is there anything else you'd like to see?" If the answer is "No," you say "Thank you" and leave with a smile. Even if you think it didn't go well, don't leave the audition looking defeated.

- Whether your audition was good or bad, the only question to ask yourself is, "Did I do my best?" Then, forget about it. Learn from your mistakes, pat yourself on the back and get ready for the next one.

- Don't take auditions personally.

- Auditioning is like catching a bus. If you miss this one, you'll get the next one.

- Always stay positive.

Start with commercials

When your agent or manager begins sending you out for auditions, chances are it will be for commercials first. Not that any medium is easy to break into, but of all of them, commercials tend to give more actors their start. As I said in the Talent chapter, you should take a commercial acting class and an improvisation class to help prepare you for commercial auditions.

Auditioning for and booking a few commercials will help you work your acting muscle as well as get your much-desired SAG card. Many of today's TV and film stars got their start in commercials. Landing a commercial that showcases your acting as well as your personality can get you some attention from theatrical casting directors and feature film directors.

When I was an agent and casting director, I saw many unknown actors book commercials that lead to a theatrical career. One in particular was a young actor I discovered at the Tisch School of the Arts. His name was Daniel Sweeney, later changed to D.B. Sweeney.

D.B. was a serious, well-trained actor who wanted to do films, but he was having trouble getting seen. As his agent, I suggested that he let me start submitting him for commercials. At first he refused, saying he didn't "do" commercials. Even back then, being a commercial actor wasn't as well respected as being a film actor. But I convinced D.B. that it could help him get his start and lead to bigger and better opportunities…and it did.

A casting director called me looking for an actor who could handle a lot of dialogue for an Army commercial. I sent D.B. to the audition and he booked it. The commercial was very popular at the time and gave him enormous exposure. Suddenly, I was getting calls from casting directors and even prominent film directors wanting to meet him. Doors opened up and he was soon auditioning for theatrical projects. He eventually starred in a few popular films in the late '80s and early '90s, including *Eight Men Out* and *The Cutting Edge*.

The point is; when you're starting out, be willing to search for your acting work opportunities anywhere and everywhere. They are out there and the more work you do on your own, the more professional opportunities will open up for you.

WORK PERSEVERANCE WITH YOUR CAG

There will be times when you'll need some help persevering with the "business" side of show business: marketing, promoting, everything you need to do to get your foot in the door. This type of work can be isolating, making you feel alone in your quest, especially when you're not feeling inspired. It can be daunting... and that's a great time to call on your support group, your Call to Action Group.

The other actors in your CAG aren't just there to help you build your Talent, boost your Confidence and help you find your type. They're also there to help you persevere.

Remember, your CAG is comprised of people with varying levels of experience. There are some actors in your CAG that will be just starting out on the acting path and others who have spent years on the journey. These newer actors will be there to take the first steps of this career work with you. Those with more experience will be there for you to draw on for knowledge, advice and understanding. If by some chance you're the most experienced in the group, let those newer members give you some fresh perspective and a jolt of energy to inspire you in your Perseverance work.

Your CAG will be there to help you keep your spirits up. Your CAG will also help you set tasks, accomplish goals, and focus on doing the grunt work...persevering.

Exercise: What have you done for your career this week?

Once again, find a good location with comfortable chairs and make sure to have room to write and do some busy work.

For these Perseverance-related CAG gatherings, I suggest setting up a regular meeting time, once a week, either at the same place or alternating, depending on your preference. You will need to set a regular meeting time to help you stay accountable for your own personal work as well as the work you're doing for the group. So make sure to find a specific day and time that everyone can meet (and stay committed to).

These meetings will require a lot of discussion about the business of the business, from headshots to agents, casting directors to auditions, and so on. The main question at these Perseverance meetings will be:

"What have you done for your career this week?"

The purpose of these meetings is to work *together* to tackle some of these Perseverance tasks and to make them a little less tedious and a lot more fun. It's always easier to pass the time and get through this work when you can talk with some friends. Your CAG is about motivating each other, setting goals and following through with career work each and every week.

If you want, each time you meet, you can have a specific topic. The two most important tasks you should be doing in the meeting, however, are **goal-setting** and **information gathering**.

• **Goal setting:** Use the first CAG meeting to discuss each of your goals out in Hollywood as specifically as you can. Everyone's *overall* goal will be to become a successful actor. Each member of your CAG will be at a different stage and therefore have different *personal* goals for their career.

Talk about these individual goals (they can be getting an agent, auditioning, landing your first acting job, etc.). Then discuss what work needs to be done for each of you to obtain these individual goals.

You're now going to set weekly plans for yourself and for each other: tasks you can do each week to help you reach your individual goals. You should discuss your plans with the CAG, take advice and verbalize exactly what you're going to do that week. Also, write it down in your Actor's Journal. This will hold you responsible for the work. Each week, be sure to talk about what you accomplished as well as next week's individual tasks and goals.

For example, if your goal is to get an agent, maybe your weekly goals look like this:

> Week 1: Research headshot photographers.
> Week 2: Schedule meetings with photographers.
> Week 3: Get headshots and feedback.
> Week 4: Pick your headshot, get them produced and copied.
> Week 5: Prepare your resume.
> Week 6: Buy labels and do agent mailing.

As you can see, ideally, by week six, you'll have put out your first agent mailing. If you can expedite this process, more power to you. But don't rush the process...you don't want to put out a sloppy product.

This Perseverance work that you set for yourselves each week will be a goal sheet that you can refer back to when you need to feel motivated. Use following meetings to keep track of your week-to-week progress.

• **Information gathering:** This is where the CAG can be the most practical, useful and fun. Have each member of the CAG do their own research and then bring it to the meeting for everyone to share.

Research includes everything from watching TV shows to tracking who's casting what, information on agents and managers, what you read in the industry trades, notes from industry functions and workshops, telling each other about auditioning experiences, etc.

You can also have special nights that are devoted to specific themes and tasks. Here's a list of some activities you can do at your CAG meeting, but try to think of more on your own. Even after you've completed these activities, continue to set new goals and come up with new themes.

CAG meeting themes

• **Headshots:** Startbygatheringinformationandresearchingvarious headshot photographers. Compare notes and recommendations on different photographers and their price packages, as well as what to expect in the photo session itself. For women, use it as a chance to share referrals on hair stylists and makeup artists. Use your CAG to help you decide what kind of looks your headshots should showcase. After you've done your photo session, use the CAG to help you pick out the best shots to use.

• **Mailings:** Get your envelopes, stamps, labels, headshots and resumes, your agent, manager or casting director books, and do your mailing together. These mailings can often be boring, so working with a group will make the time (and the task) go much quicker. Plus, it's a great time for you to chat, commiserate or gossip about the business while you stuff, stamp and lick your envelopes.

• **Monologues:** Although not a substitute for working with your acting coach, your CAG is a great place to try out and practice any new material, especially before your agent/manager meeting. Have a "Monologue Night" where everyone performs their pieces and gets feedback from the group.

• **Demo reel footage:** It's tough to really critique your own acting. If you have enough footage and you're putting together a demo reel, have your CAG take a look at your work. They can be instrumental in helping you pick out scenes in those independent or student films that best showcase you and your Talent.

• **Self-producing:** If you have an idea for a project you'd like to self-produce, who better to pitch it to then your CAG? Who knows...you might have a director with a camera in your group or an aspiring screenwriter or even a techie who can edit a film on their Mac. Have brainstorming sessions and see what you can come up with, whether it's a sketch, a short film, whatever. Go through the process of putting together a project and self-producing from start to finish.

NEVER STOP PERSEVERING

I'm sure you've heard that once you get the ball rolling and start booking a few jobs, your career can snowball pretty quickly. It is true...work begets work. BUT, you can't sit back and rely on that to happen. Use the positive energy of booking your *last* job to propel you to book your *next* job.

You must be diligent in your pursuit of more and more work. You must continue to audition, to market, to study, to work with your agent and manager on your career goals. Part of being an actor is accepting that there will always be work and that you must always persevere.

Beyond just the physical work, there is also a mentality behind Perseverance. It starts with being...

"Consciously Oblivious"

In my book "The Eight Characters of Comedy," I use a phrase as a personality trait for the character of the Lovable Loser. I call it being "**consciously oblivious.**" It describes how the character desperately wants something so bad that they will consciously put blinders on in order to achieve their Want.

Being consciously oblivious can also apply to your acting career. To be a successful actor, you need to put all your attention on your goals and block out the negative influences around you: competition, family and relationship distractions, personal drama and the discouraging aspects of the business (more on this in Section Two).

Set your sights on your goal, invest in your dream and become consciously oblivious to the obstacles. You know that they exist, but you choose not to let them get in your way. Focusing on what you want to accomplish will help you ignore the forces that are pulling at you and it will help you persevere.

It's like a thoroughbred racehorse that is fitted with blinders to help keep them focused on the finish line, avoid distractions and ultimately run faster. Being consciously oblivious helps you ignore the obvious risks, challenges and obstacles and focus on your Want. It's a positive twist on being in denial.

Being consciously oblivious means essentially not letting the frustrations all actors go through affect you as much. It means training yourself to "let go" of that bad audition, all the competition you're facing, those weeks without a call from your agent or the fact that you're waiting tables to pay the bills.

Instead, it means focusing on how you can prepare for the next audition, how you can separate yourself from the competition, what you can do to help your agent get you out on more auditions, and how you can use the money from your serving job toward your career. It's about turning negative thoughts into a positive perspective.

It means making yourself and your career a top priority. It means investing in yourself, which is ultimately empowering and will help you persevere. When you invest in yourself, you are taking complete control of your destiny.

Think of your career like starting your own business. As any business owner will tell you, at the initial stages, you invest a lot of time, work, money and energy. You need to pay attention to that investment all the time, above and beyond anything else. An acting career is the same way.

You are the most important asset you can invest in. When I opened my acting studio, I had 10 students and nobody knew who I was. People said I was crazy to try and launch a studio in a town filled with acting coaches. They weren't wrong, but I knew what I wanted: to be a successful acting coach. I put my blinders on and only concentrated on my goal...I chose to be consciously oblivious. That doesn't mean I didn't have a balanced life. It just means that when it came to my career, I was willing to invest in myself and work through the Obstacles that stood in my way. I believed in myself and in my Want.

Throughout Section One, I've talked a lot about positive thinking. Being consciously oblivious will help you get on and stay on the positive path. If you make a choice to release or change the negative influences in your life, and you stay focused on your goal and investing in yourself, then you will find yourself in a positive space.

Perseverance means being a lifer

A career in Hollywood is a marathon, not a sprint. You have to come to L.A. knowing that you will work hard for many years before you reach the finish line. That's why it's so important to enjoy the process.

It's like any other major career, be it sports, medicine or law. If you want to be the best district attorney in the city, it doesn't happen overnight. You have to go to school, compete to get in a good post-grad program, study hard, work internships, and then build up both your career and your reputation as a lawyer over several years. Acting is no different.

If you make the commitment, I promise you it will pay off. I have seen it happen time and time again. Just as I have seen some very talented people get burned out, frustrated and quit, I have seen the hard-workers who persevere eventually get their break. It's almost as if the universe at some point says, "Okay, you've stayed in the game and taken everything I've thrown at you, so here it is…take it, it's yours!"

Dylan Walsh is an actor who epitomizes the idea of being a lifer. I represented Dylan in the mid-1980s when he was first getting started. At the time, I had a very specific program for how to get someone like Dylan *seen*. Being a trained actor, it didn't take long for Dylan to book commercials, co-star roles and eventually his big break in the '80s sex romp *Loverboy*. That film lead Dylan to even more independent films, guest star roles on TV shows and supporting roles in feature films. It would take 10 more years, though, for this hard-working actor to experience the great commercial success he deserved as Dr. Sean McNamara on the FX show *Nip/Tuck*. Dylan was and still is a lifer.

You have to be a lifer. You have to be in it for the long haul. You have to have Persistence and Patience in the Pursuit of your Purpose…*always!*

On top of that, you have to enjoy your *life*. Being a lifer in this business doesn't mean that acting is the *only* thing in your life. You need to have relationships, experiences, family, charity and community work, etc. You need to expose yourself to different cultures and all forms of art. All of these will make you a more interesting and enriched person and artist.

If you have other things in your life, it will relieve some of the pressure of this business, help you enjoy the process, and keep you positive that all your hard work will pay off.

Having a full life will make you a better actor. You need to have those life experiences to draw upon. They will enrich your characterizations, your emotional depth, intellect, life perspective and imagination.

Having a full life will also help opportunities come your way. When they do, you have to be grateful. Gratitude is a key to happiness. You have to say, "Thank you!" to the universe.

Persevering will make you lucky

The word **"luck"** is thrown out there a lot, especially in Hollywood.

You hear it time and time again: "Oh, he was just lucky...to get that call, that meeting, that audition, that role." Or worse yet, when the actors themselves say, "I guess I was just lucky!"

In fact, many would suggest that all you need to make it in Hollywood is luck, that it's strictly a numbers game and a matter of being in the right place at the right time.

Actually, there is something to luck. I do believe in the idea of luck when it comes to our *individual lives*. We experience luck every day. Luck is when you win the lottery or when you avoid injury in a serious accident. Luck is when you're speeding and you zoom by a cop just as he looks away. Luck is a cosmic blend of fate, karma and forces beyond your control leading you to (or helping you avoid) certain life paths, choices and events that will ultimately propel you to your destiny.

When it comes to your acting career, however, luck is very different. In your career, luck is something that *you can help shape*. You can bring luck on to yourself by putting out positive intentions. Positive intentions bring positive outcomes. For an actor pursuing an acting career:

Luck is when *preparation* meets *opportunity*.

Write that down in your Actor's Journal. Read it again. In fact, say it out loud. This is a mantra I use and truly believe in. I've seen proof of it through the years. I've seen so many actors create their own luck simply by working hard, by being ready, by persevering.

If you work hard, *luck will come your way*. So you better be *prepared*.

At some point, you will get an opportunity to meet the right people, audition for the perfect role, and book the job that will launch your career. You owe it to yourself and all the hard work you've done to be ready for the occasion.

Let me give you a concrete example of what I mean. An actor in my class told a story about a producer who came into his restaurant, where he was waiting tables. This actor had been working hard at his career for a few years. He was devoted to his training and he was always auditioning.

He got to talking with the producer about his acting career. The producer liked him and thought he was perfect for a role on his show. He called him in to audition the next day. The actor went home, got his sides, worked on his material, coached with me early the next morning, and went to the meeting completely prepared. He booked the role.

As my student told this story in class, another student said, "Boy, were you lucky!"

That's not luck. That actor was prepared for when the opportunity presented itself and that preparation paid off.

Luck is when *preparation* meets *opportunity*.

Luck starts with you putting it out there, stating exactly what you Want, what your goal is. You declare it to yourself, your friends, your family, your acting coach, the universe. It can be anything from your overall goal of being a successful actor to more individual goals like getting an agent or landing a good audition. You tell everyone, you make that goal your top priority, and you put yourself in the mindset that you WILL accomplish that goal.

Then you work hard, you persevere, you prepare yourself to reach that goal. You do so by studying your craft, honing your Talent and building your Confidence. The more you prepare -- physically, mentally and emotionally -- the more open you are to the possibility of an opportunity (and the more ready you are when those opportunities come your way).

Opportunities *will* present themselves. Unfortunately, it's difficult to predict *when*. Timing is the one variant in luck that you can't control. If you constantly work hard, prepare yourself and open yourself up to opportunities, the less the timing will matter. You will be ready to succeed no matter where and when your lucky break occurs.

Once you accept the notion that you can create and orchestrate your own luck, it puts your destiny back into your own hands. You have the power to be prepared for when opportunity strikes. You have the power to take advantage of any and all opportunities. You have the power to be lucky. Because you produce your own luck... you'll never be out of luck.

Perseverance = Passion + Drive

To persevere, you need to have passion and drive.

Managers, agents, casting directors, producers, those in the business who have great passion and drive, will always look for those same qualities in actors. You need to have the passion for your craft as well as the drive for your career. You need to have that passion and drive running through you at all times.

Whether it's taking an acting class, auditioning or spending 14 hours a day shooting a modified, low-budget, SAG-deferred, independent film, you have to love what you're doing! Acting needs to excite you, drive you, give you a rush that you can't feel with anything (or anyone) else. You need to love being in the Acting Zone and feed off that at all times. Your passion for acting can go a long way in helping to keep you driven, helping you persevere.

Tying it all together

Talent. Confidence. Perseverance. Those are the Three Steps to Success, and you need all three working in harmony. You can't take any of these steps out of the equation.

You need the Talent and the Confidence in your Talent as well as the Perseverance to start your career, maintain and stay in the game.

If you keep working your Talent, it will boost your Confidence. The more Confidence you have, the more likely you are to persevere. The more Perseverance you have, the more you will see your Talent and Confidence grow.

All of these steps continuously work off each other. They create a positive cycle of success, which helps you reach your fullest potential as an actor. When you combine your Perseverance with your Talent and Confidence, there will be no stopping you in achieving your Want. There will be no stopping you from becoming a successful actor!

As you move on to Section Two, remember that working on these Three Steps to Success consistently will not only help you make it in Hollywood, it will also help you avoid the Three Steps to Failure.

SECTION
TWO

OBSTACLES

For every Want, there is an Obstacle.

As discussed in Section One, when it comes to your acting work, it is important to first identify what is driving your character in a scene, what is their Want. Then you must acknowledge what is standing in their way, what is blocking them from achieving that Want, what are their **Obstacles**.

Once again, the same is true for your acting career. For every Want, there is an Obstacle. Actually, when it comes to pursuing an acting career in Hollywood, for every Want, there are *several* Obstacles. For as much as you want to be a successful actor, there will always be a number of forces that will try to get in your way.

These Obstacles are barriers that come between you and your goals…and they take on many different shapes. They present themselves when you're not focused or when you're stressed, depressed, frustrated, upset or confused. Obstacles hinder your progress and detract you from your destiny. Obstacles will lead you off the path to success and onto the road to **self-sabotage**.

At its core, self-sabotage means doing anything within your power to either harm yourself or hamper your efforts. It's a form of subversion that can directly apply to a goal. When an actor succumbs to Obstacles in their career, it makes it harder to focus, to stay committed, to follow the Three Steps to Success.

Obstacles will cause you to self-sabotage. More specifically, Obstacles will stop you from going to acting class. They will impede you from getting that agent or they will lead you to actions that will cause you to lose that agent. Obstacles will cause you to miss opportunities and perform poorly at auditions. They will cause you to be unprofessional, unmotivated and unsure about yourself and your career.

Obstacles will affect you physically, mentally and spiritually. They will drain your Talent, destroy your Confidence, and cripple your Perseverance.

Obstacles only lead to a negative result. That's the difference between Obstacles and *challenges*. Actors need challenges to grow in their work (and in their lives). You set up challenges for yourself and you work to get past them in order to accomplish something positive. To accomplish your Want of having a successful acting career, you need to study, get headshots, land an agent, book a few roles, etc. Each of these is a challenge or small goal you set up for yourself to help you achieve your greater goal. Challenges produce opportunities.

While you can certainly learn a lot and even find opportunities from overcoming Obstacles, they are often potentially dangerous to you and your career. What's worse is that we often *invite* these Obstacles into our lives. We set them up for ourselves, whether consciously or unconsciously…and then we get trapped.

In order to be a successful actor, you need to identify these Obstacles. You need to recognize the most threatening Obstacles in your own *personal* career path and where they originate. Then you must do everything in your power to avoid them. If you do find yourself facing an Obstacle, you must find the strength to work through it and eventually overcome it.

Just as it's important to acknowledge your Talent, Confidence and Perseverance, you must also first acknowledge the Obstacles that could stand in your way.

In my experience, the most prevalent Obstacles an actor faces can be broken down into three distinct categories. These are the three ways that actors most commonly self-sabotage, the three biggest roadblocks and pitfalls in the path to a successful career.

The Three Steps to Failure

Distractions
Addictions
Wrong Actions

Distractions are the most difficult Obstacles that actors face. Whether it's money issues, family members, relationships or other career responsibilities, Distractions can detour actors off their path.

Addictions can be the most destructive of the Obstacles because they not only hinder your career, but also damage your life. In a town and a career where comfort and stability do not come easy, Addictions can be a tempting trap.

Wrong Actions are Obstacles you take on that can have an immediate and profound negative effect on your career. They are choices you make that can ruin your reputation, sabotage opportunities, and prevent you from moving forward in your career.

For the rest of Section Two, I will discuss Distractions, Addictions and Wrong Actions. I will show you what you can do to overcome these Obstacles. I will help you avoid The Three Steps to Failure.

First, we need to know where they come from and why.

FEAR

I had a student in my 10-week Acting Intensive class who was a very good actor. He had the Talent, the Confidence and the Perseverance. I'll call him Tom.

At the end of the 9th class, I handed everyone a short monologue to work on for the final night. Throughout the course, Tom and the other actors learned specific acting tools and techniques to help them bring scenes and monologues to life.

At the last class, I was excited to see everybody's final work, especially Tom's. He had "arced" several times over the 10 weeks, making significant strides in his acting as well as his ability to bring his own essence and personality to the material.

With his strong build, intense look and deep emotion, I gave Tom a monologue that was perfect for him. I looked forward to seeing what he would bring to the role of a young soldier back from Iraq telling his story of what "really happened" over there.

When Tom performed his scene in class, his natural instincts, acting training and intellectual understanding of the material were clearly showcased. He understood the text, the character's Want and Obstacle, as well as the tone of the piece.

Unfortunately, Tom's monologue never came to life. He brought no subtext, depth or real emotional connection to the work. It was clear that he hadn't done enough preparation. When I asked Tom specific questions about his character, he came back with vague answers. Tom finally confessed that even though he had the piece for a week, he "hadn't really worked on it."

Tom said that after he read the monologue, he loved it and instantly related to the character. He wrote down notes of what he wanted to do with the material and was excited about performing. He had even hoped that he could use this piece for an upcoming agent meeting.

When it came time for Tom to work on the monologue over the week, something would inevitably come up (girlfriend problems, roommate problems, job problems). He found himself constantly putting it off until the next day. In fact, he waited until just two hours before class to really prepare.

I said to him, "But I thought you loved the piece, that you identified with it, and were excited about performing it."

Tom replied sheepishly, "I know, I know." Then he shrugged and said, "I guess I'm just lazy."

I said, "No, you're not lazy. You're fearful."

As you can imagine, Tom was caught off guard by my response. As a proud young man, he didn't take it well when I told him he was afraid. I explained to him and the class that there really aren't *lazy* actors, just *fearful* actors. I told them that laziness is just an excuse, a guise, a cover used to hide what's really going on...**Fear**.

As artists, we have chosen a vocation where Fear runs rampant. Fear can control everything from our day-to-day activities to our destinies. As I've mentioned in Section One, actors have no clear path, no certain future, no stability...and that can breed Fear. Because of that Fear, we all have the ability and the potential to sabotage our careers.

I've seen many actors do just that. I've seen actors consciously put off studying and honing their acting craft. I've seen actors talk themselves out of career opportunities. I've seen actors make excuses for not doing what they came out to Hollywood to do. I've seen actors let various Distractions and Addictions get in their way. I've seen actors take all kinds of Wrong Actions. I've seen actors let their beautiful, innate acting Talent wither and die. I've seen actors quit, never fulfilling their destiny.

This all comes from Fear. It is Fear that will stand in the way of achieving your Want of becoming a successful actor.

Fear is a broad topic. There have been hundreds of books, dissertations, articles, seminars and a plethora of *Oprah* episodes tackling the complexities of Fear. I'm not a psychiatrist and I don't pretend to be one (though I've spent many years on the couch tackling my own Fears). Through many years of working in this industry, I can attest, however, to how Fear plays an active role in the lives of actors.

What is Fear?

Fear is the anticipation of something terrible. Fear is anxiety and a lack of courage that causes trepidation about everything we do.

Fear is the enemy of ambition. Fear paralyzes us and drives us to inaction. Even worse, Fear drives us to actions that will be destructive to our lives and our careers.

For you actors, Fear permeates throughout both your craft and your career. Fear is a lingering feeling that all actors share in some way, shape or form. Actors fear that they're not good enough, that pursuing a career will be too much of a struggle, that they won't be able to accept the changes an acting career will bring to their lives. Those are just a few examples (I'll get to more later).

Unfortunately, you have to experience Fear in order to overcome it and achieve success. Only when you face your Fears can you experience positive outcomes. You need to push yourself to take risks, to overcome Obstacles, to confront those things that are holding you back and get past them. If you don't face your Fears, they will consume you and you will fail.

Think of someone skydiving for the first time. Regardless of how much that person wants to experience the thrill and how much they have prepared for this moment, there will be some Fear leading up to the actual jump. In fact, there can be so much Fear that they may even second-guess whether they actually *want* to jump. At that point, they have a big decision to make. If they back out, they won't experience that thrill of jumping or that satisfying feeling of accomplishment. If they muster up their strength and courage and take the leap, they will have a life experience they can be proud of.

Now, apply it to an acting career. There will be times when you will have a meeting with an agent or an audition for the perfect role. You will inevitably experience some nerves and Fear before these career opportunities. You might fear that you won't impress the agent or that you'll forget your lines in the audition.

Once again, you will be faced with a choice. For some actors, that Fear can overwhelm them and they'll sabotage themselves. They'll be late for the agent meeting or they won't properly prepare for the audition. They won't face their Fear and the result will be a negative effect on their career.

The right choice is to acknowledge that you have Fear and decide that you're not going to let it get in your way. You need to make the choice to work past it, envision a positive outcome, and then...make the jump. I promise you that when you do, you will be satisfied with the result. When you face, experience and overcome your Fear, only good things *will* happen.

You have to always remember that Fear is just a feeling...not a fact. As you learn to embrace and integrate your Fear, it will lose its power to dictate your actions. You need to change your definition of Fear to "anticipatory excitement." If you did not feel Fear in this business, then it would not be your heart's desire. Fear is never going anywhere, so you have to decide how you relate to Fear.

The rest of this chapter will examine where Fear comes from and why actors have certain fears. This chapter and the rest of Section Two will help you acknowledge your Fear, addressing specific Obstacles (Distractions, Addictions, Wrong Actions). I will show you how you can get trapped by those Obstacles and how you can use your Talent, Confidence and Perseverance to get past them or avoid them altogether.

First, we need to do a little self-analysis once again. We need to examine and break down your personal Fears. That starts with discovering where your Fear originates.

WHERE DOES FEAR COME FROM?

Just like Talent, Confidence and Perseverance…we are all born with a certain amount of Fear. Whatever Fear we are predisposed to from our ancestors, relatives and DNA makeup, our own individual Fears really develop mainly through our upbringing.

Fear is instilled in us throughout our childhood. We learn about Fear and *what* we Fear from our parents, siblings, teachers, friends and most of all, through our individual childhood experiences. The way we are raised and what we learn and experience in the world around us shapes how much Fear we have and how willing we are to overcome that Fear.

Did you have parents who encouraged you to take risks, to learn from your mistakes, to overcome your Fears? Did you have parents who, because of their own life circumstances, discouraged you from trying new things, breaking through Obstacles or confronting challenges? Were there any specific circumstances or events in your upbringing that scarred you, that contributed to your Fear?

Let's try and get a handle on how much Fear you experienced in your upbringing. Once again, looking back will help you identify some of the Fears you may have translated to your acting career today. Look closely at your childhood and try and answer the following questions:

• **Were you afraid of what others thought of you?** Were you the kid who always wanted to be liked? Were you afraid to do what you wanted to do for fear that others would think of you negatively? Did you always go along with the crowd to avoid making waves? Did you take it to heart when others criticized you? Were you overly sensitive to feedback from teachers and coaches?

• **Were you afraid that you weren't good enough?** Were you too afraid to participate, whether it was an activity, project or task because you were afraid that you wouldn't be able to do the job right? Did your fear of failing stop you from even trying?

• **Were the expectations too high?** Did you set excessively high expectations for yourself? Did you show signs of being a perfectionist? Did others have high expectations of you? Did you fear letting others down? Did you fear letting yourself down?

• **Were you punished if you didn't do the job right?** Were you reprimanded and put down when you made a mistake? Were you made to feel bad if you didn't accomplish the task at hand? Were you told that you were a disappointment?

• **Were you overly protected?** Were you held back from taking risks, discovering things on your own, or learning from your mistakes? Were you sheltered and insulated from the harsh realities of disappointment, rejection and failure?

• **Were you discouraged from asserting yourself?** Were you ridiculed or told to "be quiet" when expressing your own opinions and feelings? Were your own individual thoughts, ideas and ambitions suppressed as a child? Were you told, "You can't do it?" Were you told, "Don't ask why?"

• **Did your achievements go unrecognized?** Were you not rewarded or even acknowledged for completing projects, accomplishing tasks or reaching goals? Were you deprived of the reassurance that you did a good job? Were your achievements ignored or even worse, dismissed?

After you answer these questions about your childhood, you need to examine how many of your answers still apply today. Chances are many of them still play a factor in the Fear you have as an adult. Do you still worry about what others think of you? Do you still feel like you're "not good enough?" Do you still feel the pressure of expectations from both yourself and from others?

Fear is such a challenge for it takes root at birth, grows through childhood and blossoms in adulthood. All people, especially actors, face the challenges that Fear brings.

The Two Types of Fear

The Fear that you experience in your life will translate into the Fear you experience in your acting career. Over the years, I have seen two distinct types of Fear that actors face:

The Fear of Failure/The Fear of Success

Both kinds of Fear show themselves in many different ways. Both emerge more than you would think and both are equally powerful. As you will see, some actors have more of a Fear of Failure while others have more of a Fear of Success, but all actors experience both.

No matter how much Talent, Confidence and Perseverance you've developed, there will always be an underlying Fear of being rejected, humiliated, shamed and falling flat on your face. Equally, there will always be a Fear of the new challenges and the inevitable change that success will bring. For many actors, it becomes easy to see the possibilities of failure as well as the difficulties of success.

Regardless of what stage of your career you're in, both Fear of Failure and Fear of Success can strongly influence, if not dictate, how you go about starting, pursuing and sustaining your acting career.

FEAR OF FAILURE

Fear of Failure is simply a fear that you are going to fail at something you want to achieve. Failure can mean different things to different people. Therefore, you need to figure out for yourself what it means to fail and why you're afraid to fail.

Your Fear of Failure can be as varied as your fear of flunking a test to never experiencing true love to not accomplishing your lifelong dream. Your reasons for fearing failure might be humiliation, embarrassment, abandonment, etc.

Embarking on an acting career is a daunting venture, and you are all consciously aware of that fact as you enter into it. Before you set foot in this business, you will already have an inherent Fear of Failure.

It's like a soldier going off to war. There are expectations of danger, that they might find themselves in battle, in harm's way. The soldier knows that going in and naturally fears that risk. As actors, you all know that there are many more actors who fail than those that "make it." So you fear *that* risk.

There are other ways a Fear of Failure plays into your acting career that go well beyond an overall Fear of not being successful. A Fear of Failure also plays into the rejection you face, the pressures of this business, the expectations of your family, and how you perceive yourself. The Fear of Failure can be the ever-present feeling that pursuing an acting career was the wrong choice.

I have identified seven different factors that fall under the Fear of Failure. These are all crippling fears that, unfortunately, most actors share. The problem is that many of these fears relate to each other. They build off one another, deepening that overall Fear of Failure. Some of you might experience these fears to varying degrees, but it's important to look at each of them closely and see which ones apply to your life and career.

Seven Fear Factors Of Failure

1. You fear you're not good enough. Every actor has felt this before, even the greats. There is always that lingering feeling that we're simply not good enough...not smart enough, not pretty enough, not skinny enough, not talented enough, etc. Most actors who struggle with feeling "not good enough" in their personal life most certainly bring it into their acting career. They will compare themselves to other actors, feel that they don't belong in Hollywood, or fear that they're not cut out for this business.

2. You fear you will disappoint your family. It's important for many of us to make our family proud of who we are and what we're doing with our lives. You fear what your family will think if you're not successful. Nobody wants to let their family down, especially if they're supportive of you and your career, whether its encouragement or even financial help. A family's high hopes can put unnecessary pressure on you to succeed as an actor, to show them that their support isn't going to waste.

3. You fear your family will be proved right. Many actors choose not to follow the career path their parents set out for them. They choose to ignore their advice, to go against their wishes, and pursue this dream. They come out to Los Angeles with no emotional or financial support from their family. All they have is a desire to prove them wrong. The Fear is…what if they're right? There is a Fear that if they fail, they will have to admit defeat, suffer the humiliation, face their family, and prepare for the inevitable "I told you so."

4. You fear your own expectations. You have high expectations that you set for yourself in Hollywood. You've got a clear vision for your future, you've planned out a career path, and the idea of not reaching your goals can be crushing. You're afraid that if you fail you will *really* feel like a failure. You're afraid that you will let *yourself* down.

5. You fear you're sacrificing a stable life. Many of us are taught at a young age that life goes as follows: school, college, job, marriage, better job, mortgage, kids, promotion, savings, retirement. An acting career doesn't really follow that pattern (or any pattern for that matter). Whether you're 21, 31 or 41, there is always that Fear in the back of your mind that you're letting that "planned" path go by the wayside. You're sacrificing the lifelong stability that path offers while you take a risk on a career that might not have much of a reward.

6. You fear you're missing other career opportunities. Chances are there is something else that you excel at, another talent or skill you possess. You fear that you might be giving up other opportunities at success while you pursue this acting dream. Maybe you could have been a writer, an architect, an athlete, a designer, etc. It's a Fear that you made the wrong career decision in your life...and hoping you never have to look back and say, "What if?"

7. You fear you'll never be a star. You fear that you won't get your chance in the spotlight. You fear that, for whatever reason, you'll never have your day in the sun. You'll always be a background player, an extra or, at best, a day player. You fear that you'll never really get a chance to shine and show people your full potential.

Along with a Fear of Failure comes a **Fear of the Unknown.** It's a fear that you don't know what to expect with an acting career or a life in Hollywood. As such, you won't be able to fully prepare yourself and you will inevitably fail.

We've all seen, heard or read how Hollywood can be a chaotic, high stakes, unpredictable place where anything can happen -- that can be overwhelming. The Fear of the Unknown is a Fear that you won't be able to keep up with this fast-paced industry, that you will be unprepared and unequipped for the opportunities that will come your way.

Not giving 100 percent

A Fear of Failure makes you afraid of what people might think of you. It puts too much pressure on you to succeed, breaking down your self-worth. Worst of all, this Fear can make you unwilling to work or try as hard.

When it comes to acting or career work, many actors aren't willing to invest 100 percent -- physically, mentally or emotionally. Once again, it has nothing to do with them being lazy or less ambitious...they're fearful. Not putting 100 percent into their work safeguards them from both their conscious and subconscious Fear of Failure.

Many actors feel that if they put 100 percent of their time, energy and passion into their class work, auditions and career, and they fail...the fall will be harder to take. They fear the ramifications of failure -- humiliation, embarrassment, abandonment.

Therefore, some actors will only invest about 50 percent. The idea is, the less they invest, the lesser the fall -- and the hurt, pain or embarrassment -- if they fail. They can save face and simply say, "I didn't give it my all." This misguided philosophy runs rampant among many actors in Los Angeles who prevent themselves from committing fully to their careers. Over time, these actors won't even put in the 50 percent. They'll stop trying altogether. At that point, it's time to pick a new career.

You can't be afraid to fail. You need to keep in mind that, at the very least, you will always learn something from failing. We often learn just as much (if not more) from our failures than our successes.

You need to give it your all or nothing will happen. No risk... no gain. You need to move past your Fear of Failure to have any success.

FEAR OF SUCCESS

Just as many people fear success as they do failure. You might wonder, "Who would fear being a rich, famous, successful actor?" Believe it or not, the Fear of Success can be just as prevalent as the Fear of Failure.

Many actors aren't prepared to deal with the success an acting career could bring and therefore, they fear it. Whether consciously or unconsciously, they prevent themselves from achieving their goals. In each and every actor, there is a Fear of how things would *change* if they actually did become successful.

There are new pressures and new challenges that accompany success. For many actors, this Fear starts to emerge after the initial taste of success (getting an agent, booking a job, getting noticed).

If you think back to my student Tom and his story at the beginning of the chapter, he experienced a Fear of Success. He told me that since he had been doing so well over the 10-week class and had received so much good feedback, he didn't think he could live up to the higher expectations and the pressure that came with taking his acting to the next level.

Plus, he explained that he had planned on using his monologue for an upcoming agent meeting. After listening to me talk about Fear, he realized that he was fearful of that agent meeting...but not of *failing*. Rather, he was fearful the monologue and the meeting would go *well*, and then he would have no choice (or excuse) but to go forward with his acting career. He was afraid of his potential for success and it stopped him from doing the work.

Before we tackle Fear of Success, it's important to first define what *success* means to you. Every actor has a different idea of success, whether it's to be a working actor, a life in the theatre or a big movie star. Some actors are content just making enough money to support themselves and their family while others want the fame, notoriety and a big house in the hills.

What does success mean for you in your acting career? How would "having success" change your life? Just like a Fear of Failure, this Fear of Success can take on many different shapes. It comes from pressures and expectations -- both internal and external -- as well as a preoccupation about the perceptions of others.

More than anything else, a Fear of Success stems from having to change, whether it's your status, finances, surroundings, work load, relationships or your Comfort Zone. Change is hard. Many of us fear change, and if success brings change, then we'll fear success.

I have also identified seven different factors that fall under the Fear of Success. You need to realize that just like the Seven Fear Factors of Failure, these will often build upon each other and add to your overall Fear of Success. Once again, you will experience these fears to varying degrees. Let's examine which of these fears apply to you the most.

Seven Fear Factors Of Success

1. You fear your family will steal your spotlight. There is a fear that as soon as you start getting successful, your family dynamics will change. You fear your family will want and expect more from you...and not just your immediate family, but also your "family of friends." You fear that they will try to take over your life, therefore suffocating you and your individuality. The fear is your family will overwhelm you, invade your privacy, and put more pressure on you to sustain your success. Even worse, you fear they'll try to selfishly benefit from your celebrity and success.

2. You fear you will forfeit your "bohemian lifestyle." There is a lot of poetry in the life of a struggling artist. There is a fear that if you do anything "commercial," it might ruin the integrity of your art and corrupt your creativity. You fear that success might also set you apart from your starving artist friends. You fear the repercussions that this change of status will offer, not only in your own life, but also in how others will perceive you. You might fear that your friends will envy your success or be jealous of your career.

3. You fear you will have to work harder. You fear that success might mean longer days, more commitments and less time to hang out with your friends, watch TV, play video games, or surf the Internet. No matter where you are in your life, there is a familiarity to it, a Comfort Zone. When you have to work harder, you often have to leave that Comfort Zone and that can be scary.

4. You fear you will lose your privacy. You want to be a successful actor, but you fear that you couldn't handle the scrutiny that goes along with it. You fear living your life in the public eye, having your private life out there for all to see, examine and judge. There is a fear, especially now in the YouTube generation, that anything you do or say as a public figure will be caught on tape and broadcast for millions to see. You're afraid that you will lose your anonymity and your ability to live your life as before.

5. You fear other's expectations of you. As you succeed, you *will* face higher expectations. You're afraid that you won't be able to live up to those expectations, whether they're set by your family, friends or the public. You fear letting people down. You fear that people will expect you to be brilliant *all the time*. They will expect you to always be beautiful, thin, articulate, charming or "funny like you are on TV!" It's a fear that you will always have to be "on."

6. You fear your own expectations. As we get a taste of success, we continue to set higher goals and expectations. We fear that those goals might get to be too high and we won't be able to reach them. If you do well in acting class one week, you fear you won't be able to top your performance the next week. If you receive great acclaim for your first film role, you fear how you will fare in your next role. You fear the more successful you become, the tougher it will be to maintain your success.

7. You fear that you might be a fraud. You fear you might not be as good as your acting coach, agent or even your audience believes you to be. You fear that you may have just gotten lucky. You fear that you really don't have the Talent and you aren't worthy of all the attention, accolades and great reviews. You question why this success is happening and you wonder if you really deserve it.

Fearing your potential

I know we all think that it would be fantastic to have the money, the power, the fame, the glory. However, success is also daunting for all the same reasons.

Often times…people fear their *potential* more than anything.

Just like a Fear of Failure, actors will not give 100 percent. They have this Fear of Success and it makes them procrastinate, avoid opportunities, or partake in any number of other Wrong Actions (which I'll get to in Chapter 3).

That choice to not give 100 percent can come from this Fear of Success just as much as the Fear of Failure. Actors who don't give their all have grown content with their lifestyle, reputation, expectations, ideas and plans for the future...and success would only alter those. So, the less effort they put forward, the less they have to worry about *change*.

Fear of Failure and Fear of Success are both powerful Fears that every actor has to acknowledge. That starts with identifying your own individual Fears.

Exercise: Identifying your Fear

When it comes to your career, what do you Fear?

Although this exercise is very simple, it does require you to dig deep inside yourself and be completely honest, which is difficult for many of us to do. It's a self-examination of what types of Fear you have, what types of Fear you need to get past to achieve success.

Open up your Actor's Journal and on one page, at the top, write this down:

```
If I fail, I fear...
```

Then fill up that page with random thoughts about your Fears of Failure. Simply finish this sentence as many times as you can... don't edit yourself. Write down every possible Fear that comes to mind, but don't analyze them. Don't cross off anything or dismiss any thought. Just let your thoughts flow on to the page, like a free-flowing stream of consciousness.

When you've exhausted all those Fears, turn to a fresh sheet. At the top of that one, write down:

```
If I succeed, I fear...
```

Fill up that page with your thoughts about your Fears of Success. Once again, write as much as you can and be as honest as possible. These are your personal thoughts, reflections, your personal Fears.

I did this exercise in class and afterward, I asked my students if there were any Fears they felt comfortable enough to share. Here are some Fears that my students discussed:

```
If I fail, I fear...
```

I will disappoint my parents.
I will never get anyone to love me.
I won't be able to afford things that I want.
I will waste a good portion of my life pursuing an acting career.
I'll be humiliated in front of a casting director.
I won't have enough money to even eat.
I'll have to borrow more money from my parents.
I will have to settle for a life as a waiter.
I will always wonder, "What if?"
I will turn to drinking or drugs.
I'll never realize my potential.

```
If I succeed, I fear...
```

I won't be loved for who I really am.
I won't have anyone I can really trust.
I will have more attention than I want.
My agent will expect more from me.
Friends and family will ask me for favors.
I will always have to be GREAT.
I will have to change my lifestyle.
I won't ever have privacy again.
I'll be scrutinized by others in the industry.
I will have to work much harder than I ever expected.
I'll never be as good of an actor as I'm supposed to be.

As my students started to open up and share their Fears in class, it became a very lively discussion. Although we didn't solve anyone's Fears (which was never my intention), I had a lot of my students tell me it was good to just get them out in the open.

You can also do this exercise with your CAG. If you do, follow the same process as I've instructed with all the other CAG exercises. All you'll need is a location, comfortable chairs and your Actor's Journal.

Each member will participate. On the top of one page of your Actor's Journal, write down, "If I fail, I fear..." and take five minutes to free associate and write down what comes to mind. Then turn the page over and write at the top, "If I succeed, I fear..." and do the same thing.

After 10 minutes, stop writing. You will then discuss each other's Fears and how they relate to your acting careers. Don't be afraid to keep some of your Fears and the negative events that caused those Fears private. This exercise is meant to give you a deeper understanding of what Fears may be blocking you from being a successful actor.

Nobody in your CAG should judge, critique or analyze anyone else's Fears. This is just a discussion. You will find that many of you share similar Fears and talking about them can be very illuminating.

Whether you do it on your own or with your CAG, this exercise is an opportunity for you to become more self-aware. It will open your eyes and make you consciously aware of what Fears stand in your way of being successful. If you're consciously aware of something, then you have a better chance of accepting it, confronting it, and ultimately getting past it.

One thing you'll probably notice is that you share elements of BOTH a Fear of Failure and a Fear of Success.

If you look at them closely, you'll see that Fear of Success and Fear of Failure are really just two different sides of the same internal struggle. Some may lean more toward a Fear of Failure while others lean more toward a Fear of Success. However, the two are so closely connected under the umbrella of Fear that we all have elements of both.

Most of you will start with a Fear of Failure because you haven't had that taste of success yet, at least not in your acting career. Others might start with a Fear of Success as they have experienced success before in some other aspect of their life. They've seen the change that success can bring, both the good and the bad.

Whether it's the Fear of Success, the Fear of Failure or both, this Fear impacts every single thing you do in your career, from the choices you make to the actions you take.

FACING YOUR FEAR

When you have Fear, you set up Obstacles that sabotage your career. As I mentioned in the Introduction to this section, those Obstacles come in the form of the Three Steps to Failure:

Distractions
Addictions
Wrong Actions

Each of these Obstacles is the result of Fear and the consequences of having Fear. Unfortunately, for most of us, they are a misguided, destructive and paralyzing way to deal with our Fear.

You don't need Fear. You can overcome it, and you *have to* overcome it. You have to face your Fear, experience it, and push past it. You must embrace the idea that you're stronger than your Fear. If acting is your dream and you can fight through your

Fear, then you will come out on top. I've seen it done, I've seen it happen.

Over the next few chapters, I will specifically discuss The Three Steps to Failure and how each of them comes from Fear. The point is to help you identify the ways Fear can overtake your career. I'll give you advice on how to overcome your Fear and how to get past these Three Steps to Failure to ultimately achieve great success.

THE THREE STEPS

TO FAILURE

DISTRACTIONS
ADDICTIONS
WRONG ACTIONS

CHAPTER 1
DISTRACTIONS

Distractions are the trickiest of the Three Steps to Failure because they are often the most elusive.

Distractions are tough for actors to detect both in their personal life and in their acting career because they are often comforting and familiar. As such, we don't necessarily see Distractions for what they really are…an Obstacle.

Sure, every now and then, you need to take time for yourself. You need to mentally, physically, emotionally and spiritually refresh. You need to breathe, relax, do something fun, and clear your mind of the chaos that is the "life of an actor in Hollywood."

You need to go see a movie with a date, grab coffee with a friend, spend time with your family, watch TV, read, play poker, work out, do yoga, garden, walk your dog, play with your cat, and so on. These are all healthy ways to comfort you, give you Confidence, help you recharge, and get you back to doing your life's work in a clear, positive way.

In Los Angeles, there are plenty of opportunities for you to unwind. With the ocean, mountains, desert, vineyards, museums, restaurants, bars, theatres and Las Vegas nearby, there is no shortage of ways to help you take a timeout.

BUT, be careful. These diversions are only beneficial to you and your career if used in moderation. When you spend more time at your hobbies, sight-seeing or relaxing than at your career, these diversions become Distractions, and can take a toll on your acting career.

Distractions always come down to personal choice. You have the control and the power to keep Distractions from getting in the way or sabotaging you and your goals. You simply need to always remember your purpose and priorities.

However, there are some Distractions that will appear to be out of your control. These have the potential to be the most damaging to your acting career and they come from some unlikely and unexpected sources. These are the Distractions I will discuss for the rest of the chapter.

Most common Distractions

The three Distractions most actors face are:

Money
Family
Relationships

Perhaps money is understandable as most of us have, at some point, faced financial struggles. While those with a stable career know that money will be coming in with a steady paycheck, for actors, the jobs are often few and far between...if they're working at all. There's no guarantee as to when they'll get that next paycheck. Actors, for the most part, are financially handicapped, and that lack of money can distract from any career.

But Family and Relationships?

Your parents, boyfriends, girlfriends, spouses, significant others and even your friends can all distract you from your career. Now don't jump to conclusions. I'm not going to spend this chapter telling you how you should cut off ties with your loved ones. Family and relationships are vital to having a happy, fulfilling life. However, I will show you how these positive influences can sometimes turn negative -- deterring you, pressuring you, and veering you off your career path.

You need to learn to prioritize and set boundaries when it comes to your Distractions. A successful career in Hollywood requires a great deal of focus, time and energy. You don't have time to be distracted.

WHY ARE WE DISTRACTED?

The answer is really simple:

It's safe.

Distractions pull you away from the hard work and the stress of life. What makes Distractions so enticing is that they are often something you feel more in control of, more powerful about. They're often easier than the task at hand.

You take on Distractions because they're enjoyable, they're familiar, they make you feel more at ease...even though you should be spending your time working your monologue, doing your agent mailing, or submitting yourself for online castings.

Even if these Distractions aren't necessarily comforting, you still take them on because they're easier than dealing with the hardships and the instability of your career.

Distractions come from Fear

As I discussed, your career path and life in Hollywood can be so unpredictable and unstable, it's easy to become fearful and search for something more solid and tangible to grab onto. That's where Distractions come into play. Distractions are nothing more than a safety blanket; a way for you to pull the sheets over your head and block out all the difficulties of your career.

As an actor faces highs and lows, they will consciously turn to things they feel they can control. The problem is that many actors take on too many of these Distractions. They'll spend more energy losing themselves in their Distractions ultimately because they're *fearful*. They are fearful of their potential, of the unknown, of the inevitable hard work of their acting career.

As an actor, you can't afford Distractions. You will be too busy to deal with them. You will have to explore so much unmarked territory that you can't be fearful and run away. You have to march into those places with strength, desire and an unshakable will. You don't have the time or luxury to let Fear lead you to Distractions. You have to stay on course. You have to identify and hopefully avoid these self-defeating influences, these Distractions.

MONEY

Money affects everything.

Money affects your dreams and goals, your day-to-day activities, your moods, attitudes and outlook on life. It affects *where* you live and *how* you live. Money affects your relationships -- whether with your family, friends or your partner. And yes, money will affect your acting career.

For actors, money is the most common of all the Distractions.

There are so many actors that are forced to cut their career in Los Angeles short -- before it even gets off the ground -- because they don't have enough money.

Money, or the lack thereof, is the number one reason students have to "take a break" from acting class. I have seen actors start to progress in their craft, getting to a point where they're ready to get an agent, to go audition, or even work as an actor. Then suddenly, they have to leave class and stop all that momentum they built up because they "ran out of money." They often come back a few months later, but by then their acting muscles are rusty and they have to start all over again.

If you remember from the Perseverance chapter, I said you need to come to Los Angeles with sufficient savings. No matter how much you have in the bank, though, you will find it easy to spend quickly. The cost of living is simply that much greater in L.A. than most other cities across the country (except perhaps New York), whether you're talking about apartments, cars, gas, groceries or entertainment.

Pursuing an acting career is also an expensive venture, especially when you're first getting started. Though prices are always changing with the times, you can expect to pay $300 plus for headshots and copies, at least $200 a month on acting class, and plenty of money in gas, driving to auditions and networking events. Plus, if you happen to get your SAG card, it will cost you over $2,000 just to join!

Many actors say they just can't cut it when it comes to the cost. In that way, it seems like this Distraction is really out of your control. After all, how can you focus on your acting career when you're just trying to find a way to pay the bills? How can you afford headshots or class when you're dropping all your income on that studio apartment in the Valley?

Money is a career trap

Money is the deadliest of the Distractions because it can derail you and your career for years as you try to just keep up and simply survive. For some actors, their savings run out too quickly. For others, their survival job isn't paying them enough. Still others rely too heavily on financial support from family, only to eventually have it discontinued.

No matter how much savings an actor has or how much financial support they're receiving, they need a *survival job* to supplement it. If one job isn't making ends meet, they need to get another job.

However, that raises *another* money Distraction. There are those actors who are so distracted by their survival jobs or even their other "careers" and the financial comfort they provide, that they let acting fall by the wayside.

As you can see, money affects actors in several ways.

I want to give you three examples of actors who let money distract them from their career. You'll notice in all three examples that each actor had high hopes and were very ambitious about their career...and then money problems got in the way. Chances are you'll find that you identify with one of these actors more than the others. Hopefully, that will give you a red flag to watch out for and avoid in your own pursuit.

#1 Lexi's Story

Lexi came to L.A. with $10,000 in the bank. She immediately got into acting class and progressed in her craft. After six months, however, she came to me and said, "I have to drop out of class." She hadn't gotten a survival job and her savings had dried up quicker than she thought. She had to leave class and put her career on hold.

There are those actors like Lexi who live off their savings when they move to Hollywood. Many build up their savings before moving so that they don't have to get a job right away. Rather, they think they can spend all their time focusing on building their acting career. Others are a little more naïve and simply assume their savings will last them longer than it does.

While actors like Lexi might have it good for a while, their savings will eventually dry up...often more quickly than they think. If they haven't found a new job to help supplement their savings, they'll be in trouble.

Many actors don't realize how long it takes and how much it costs to get settled and acclimated to a big city like Los Angeles. They have the unrealistic belief that they can get their big break in about six months. They don't realize that acting and adapting to life in Hollywood is a process.

Even as they continue to spend, they *still* don't get a job. They fear that a job would be a "distraction" to their acting career. Eventually, it gets to the point where they have nothing left other than an empty bank account to show for it.

They might be spending their savings on something positive for their career -- class, headshots, etc. -- but they don't balance it with a survival job. Then they *do* get distracted from their acting career...because they can't afford to continue their pursuit.

The same problem arises for those actors that are financially supported by their family. You have to assume that eventually, at some point, that funding of your career will run out. If you don't have a survival job backing up that financial support, your career will come to a screeching halt. Plus, with family supporting you, there is always that burden, that extra sense of obligation. That pressure to succeed that comes when someone else is holding the strings to the pocketbook.

Regardless of how much savings you have or how much you're being financed, be aware that it *will* run out. It will help get you started, but you need something to supplement that money. The solution? Get a survival job!

#2 Paul's Story

Paul came to L.A., got a survival job and got into acting class. After a few months and showing signs of progress in his craft, Paul told me, "I have to drop out of class." He said his survival job wasn't paying enough for him to continue and he had to take some time off from pursuing his career to make some money.

There are many actors like Paul who come to Los Angeles and actually get a survival job, but never seem to have enough money to put toward their career. They may be working, but it's still not enough to make ends meet.

While I sympathize with Paul and understand his plight, using the excuse that you don't have enough money to pursue your acting career is unacceptable.

Los Angeles is a huge city and regardless of how many actors are looking for work, there are endless opportunities for jobs. Many famous actors have gone on talk shows and chatted about their "hungry years," their "salad days," where they had to take on odd survival jobs (janitor, ditch digger, birthday clown, etc.), anything to get the money needed to continue pursuing their career. I'm not saying it will be a glamorous job, but it will pay the bills.

Not making enough money in your survival job is a legitimate Obstacle, but there is a way you can overcome it:

Get *another* survival job.

At the end of the Want chapter, you signed a contract pledging to do whatever needed to be done to make it in Hollywood. You made a commitment to yourself to work hard at achieving your goal of becoming a successful actor.

Part of that work includes your survival job, finding a way to get the money you need to fuel your hopes and dreams -- your career. You can't be afraid to work and work hard. You must be willing to work one, two or even *three* jobs! If that's what it takes to fulfill your obligation to yourself and your career, then that's what you must do.

Many actors say they don't make enough money...yet they seem to have loads of free time. Take a good, honest look at your average day, all 24 hours. If you figure eight hours of sleep and four hours of fun and relaxation, that still leaves you with 12 hours each day to divvy up for career work and survival jobs. If you multiply that by five for a normal work week, that's 60 hours you should be filling with *work*.

Successful actors are some of the hardest working employees in the workforce, especially in terms of hours they put in weekly. Whether working on a film or TV set, 14 hour days are the norm... you might as well practice for it now.

Sure you need to occasionally take time off for yourself, but if you're sitting around at home day-dreaming, spending time on MySpace or complaining to your friend how you don't have enough money, you have time to get another survival job!

#3 Marty's Story

Marty came to L.A. with his wife to finally pursue his lifelong dream of being an actor. After 15 years of working in advertising, Marty was able to get a good survival job as a part-time advertising consultant. He got into class and quickly made headway in his acting. After a year, Marty told me, "I have to drop out of class." He explained that his part-time job became a full-time job with good money, but extra responsibilities. Marty had to "once again" put his acting career on hold.

Actors like Marty, who do find financial security, will sometimes have their priorities set elsewhere. These are the actors that get wrapped up in their survival job and neglect their acting career. Or they have other full-time careers and simply don't have enough time for their acting career. There is an underlying concern or need for financial security and stability, so much so that making money is all they think about.

If you're serious about an acting career, the survival job is only there to help you....*survive*. Your survival job is only meant to fund your life and your acting career necessities.

Those actors who get wrapped up in their survival job will miss class because they have to work or miss an audition because they can't get someone to cover their shift. While I understand that we all need to make money, you need to prioritize and find a job that will be flexible and understanding to your acting needs. Trust me...they exist.

Also, if you have *another* full-time career, it will be next to impossible for you to ultimately succeed as an actor. Acting requires too much dedication and focus...it's a full-time job in itself.

An outside career inherently comes with its own responsibilities, commitments and pressures. Sure it might alleviate some of the money issues and bring stability to your life, but then you're struggling with time, which is just as valuable to an actor. Although I've seen many actors try to balance the two, more often than not it's the acting career that suffers.

Don't let your survival job or your career overshadow your acting career.

Fear leads to money Distractions

Most actors find themselves facing money Distractions at some point in the beginning stages of their acting career. Once again, the reason why comes down to Fear.

That Fear shows itself in several different ways. I want you to think back to what I talked about in the Fear chapter about investing completely in your career.

As I discussed, there is an underlying Fear in many actors of having to actually do the work involved in pursuing this dream. It goes back to that idea of having to invest 100 percent in what you're doing. Many actors misguidedly believe that if they invest in their career *completely*, the greater the risk for a fall. They find ways to avoid fully investing, and one of the excuses they use most is money.

They'll blame a lack of money for why they're not taking classes, getting headshots or even auditioning. They simply say, "I can't afford it," and that releases them from their obligation.

Other actors fear that having money will put them one step closer to facing their dream and the changes that come with it. If an actor has the money, then they have no excuse but to enter that unfamiliar territory of the acting world.

On top of that, many actors have the fear of working too hard and thus, being overwhelmed.

It's a common fear in any profession. When you're pursuing an acting career, you essentially need to work two jobs: your career work and your survival job. There will be a lot of "labor" involved and that scares many actors.

There is a fear that you, as an actor, won't be able to balance your career work with your survival job. You fear that finding time for both your career and your survival job will overwhelm you, exhaust you, stress you out, and hamper your pursuit of being an actor.

Think back to the examples we just used -- Lexi, Paul and Marty. Lexi doesn't work at all, relying solely on the savings as she pursues her career. She's fearful of taking on a survival job because it might be too much to handle and it would interfere with her acting work.

Even though Paul is working a survival job, he is fearful of the thought of working *another* survival job because the long work day would overwhelm him.

Marty actually shares the same fears of being overwhelmed and working too hard. But he has the added fear that he won't be able to *balance* his survival job/career with his acting career. With his need for stability and security, Marty chose the familiar, financial comfort of his survival job/career over his acting career.

If you're serious about your acting career, there is no excuse to let this Fear distract you. You can work and you can work hard. You can be productive with your time. You can do whatever you need to do to survive and thrive in your acting career.

Work through money Distractions

You have to trust that you won't be overwhelmed, that you're capable of working at a job (or two) and your acting career at the same time. You have to believe that you have the stamina, the strength and the drive to work a long day. You have to believe that you're ambitious enough to put in the extra hours, eager enough to learn and experience more, smart enough to organize and prioritize your life, and dedicated enough to make it all happen.

The best way to believe is to do it and witness the great things you're capable of, discovering the hard worker living inside of you.

Remember, successful actors are often some of the hardest working people in the industry. When you become a successful actor, you will work even harder than you do now...whether you have one, two or three jobs! A successful actor will wake up at dawn to work out, appear on a morning talk show, head to the TV set to film for the day and have just enough time to suit up and hit the red carpet for a Hollywood premiere. Then they'll hit the sack, ready to do it all over again the next day.

Think of this experience of working 12 hours a day on your career and your two survival jobs as preparation for the life of a successful actor.

This process of being a hard-working actor will not only rid you of money Distractions, but also help fulfill your dreams and build character, responsibility, discipline and a strong work ethic.

FAMILY

As you've seen from reading this book, there is no greater influence on you and your life than your **family**.

Family not only shapes your upbringing, personality, goals and dreams, it also shapes how you handle certain pressures, Fears and Obstacles.

Unless you've come from a destructive, abusive upbringing, I believe your families love you and tried to do their best in raising you. To begin to resolve any issues with your family, you need to first believe that they tried to give you the best upbringing they could.

With that in mind, sometimes their "best" can still leave you feeling fearful, insecure and lonely. The effects of your upbringing and the relationship that you have with your family now -- good or bad -- can also involve a lot of pressure. That pressure your family puts on you, whether consciously or subconsciously, can lead to Distractions.

While there are many ways that family can distract an actor from their career, the two most common are:

1. A Lack Of Support And Understanding

2. A Reliance On You Being The Point Person

For some actors, their family does not *support* their choice to be an actor, which puts enormous pressure on these actors to prove their family wrong. Even if their family does support them, they still might not *understand* what it takes to be an actor and that puts pressure on them as well. Having to constantly defend and explain life and career choices is a Distraction.

For other actors, their families will rely on them for everything, making them the *point person*. These actors become the one that everyone turns to in times of trouble, the shoulder to cry on, the pillar, the planner, the one that has to take care of all the family issues.

Both Distractions are equally detrimental to an actor's daily tasks as well as their overall career goals.

A Lack Of Support And Understanding

"What are you doing with your life?"

That's the question that many actors dread hearing from their mothers, fathers or any family member for that matter.

Chances are, you had to do quite a bit of convincing when you first brought up the idea of moving to Hollywood to become a struggling, out-of-work actor. I'd be willing to bet that for most of you, your family didn't understand why you would take on such a risky venture. They also probably didn't support your decision.

That lack of support from your family and the pressure that comes along with it is a Distraction. All it does is build up and reinforce your negative thoughts. You fear that your family will be proved right. You fear that you are destined to fail. You constantly question whether you made the right choice because they constantly remind you that you made the wrong choice. Your family doesn't consider "acting" a real career and they wonder when this "phase" will pass.

Family expectations and pressure can put an enormous amount of weight on an actor's shoulders. Not only is it a *physical* Distraction that keeps them from doing their career work; it's also an *emotional* Distraction that eats away at their Confidence and self-worth.

I have seen actors come into class dejected or demoralized after a simple conversation with a family member.

There was a very talented actor named Andy who began to come to class defeated and unmotivated. One day after class, I took him aside and asked him what was wrong. Andy told me that before class, he had just gotten off his weekly "what-are-you-doing-with-your-life?" phone call from his father.

He's not alone. Actors hear questions like this from their family all the time:

"What is it that you do in L.A. again?"
"Have you gotten any work?"
"Been on TV yet?"
"Is acting really a good career choice?"
"Do you *really* want to be an actor?"
"When are you going to get a *real* job?"

And, of course...

"What are you doing with your life?!"

These questions are not necessarily asked in malice. They might truly be said out of concern, with the best of intentions. That's where the lack of understanding comes in. Unless you have family members that are artists themselves, they probably don't understand the desire and need to pursue a career in the arts. They don't understand the work and sacrifices you need to make to succeed in this business.

Even if they do support you, they probably still have a number of the same concerns that come from this lack of understanding.

They worry that an acting career is not a dependable, respectable, financially stable profession...not nearly as much as a career in law, medicine, marketing or technology. They worry about the struggle, the rejection and the fact that you appear to be risking stability for a one-in-a-million chance to be a working actor.

Family expectations

Generally speaking, when it comes to career expectations, men often get more pressure from the family than women. Even though times have changed quite a bit, sociologically speaking, there is still a "male provider" mentality that is passed down from mothers and fathers to their sons.

There still seems to be an expectation for the man to get a stable job and provide for his family. While women deal with it as well, I can't tell you how many stories I hear from my male actors who experience this pressure with every career move they make.

The amount of pressure your family puts on you for following an acting career path also tends to relate to your *position* in the family.

There are several studies that explore the mysteries of birth order and how the youngest child is treated differently than the oldest and so on. I'm not going to delve too deeply into the psychology of birth order, but I can tell you that I have witnessed firsthand some of the results of these studies.

The oldest child in any family tends to get the most amount of pressure to succeed. There is often a lot more attention paid to that child than future siblings and thus, more expectations. In most families, the eldest is often the most responsible and usually picks a career that offers financial stability.

On the flip side, the youngest child tends to be the most rebellious. Interestingly enough, they are often the most artistic and the most willing to pursue an artistic career path. They don't tend to deal with as much family pressure. They are often left alone to follow their own path. They are often the social ones, the risktakers.

The middle children tend to lean either way but never as extreme as the other two. It's interesting when I bring this up in class how many of my acting students are the babies of the family or the only child.

Regardless of where you fall in your birth order, there will always be an inherent desire to appease your family. If appeasing your family is a top priority in your life, that will most definitely be a Distraction. Family pressure can make you feel defeated, tired, miserable, exhausted and even sick. You spend enough energy working on building up your own Confidence in this profession. Having to continuously justify your career choice is draining. It can deplete you of the energy needed to endure, to persevere.

Helping your family support and understand

While it's not easy to make your family understand or support your desire to be an actor, the best thing you can do to relieve some of the pressure is to *communicate* with them. Talk to them about why you *need* to be an actor as well as the complexities of the craft and business of acting. Then, show them your progress.

For many of you, your family will only have limited knowledge of what pursuing an acting career involves. As such, they'll only look at your career in black and white. Your family may only see it as "you're a working actor" or "you're not a working actor."

You need to tell them about what you do. Explain the process, the reasoning behind your career moves and how this process can help you be successful. Here are some specific ideas of what to talk to your family about:

• **Tell your family your Want.** Let them know exactly *why* you want to be an actor. Explain to them your desire, your innate ability, your need to act and entertain. Be as open and honest with them as you can. Show them why this is the career choice for you.

• **Let your family know that acting is a craft.** Like any other craft, acting requires time, patience and hard work. In order to be skilled at your craft, you need to take acting classes. Explain how acting class builds up your acting muscles, hones your skills and preps you for auditions, which will eventually lead to work.

• **Talk to your family about your career work.** Explain how headshots are your calling cards in this business and thus a necessary expense. Educate them on what agents and managers do and how they are vital to opening doors and getting you opportunities to succeed. Explain the importance of casting director workshops for networking and making industry contacts. Tell them how joining a theatre company can keep you working at your craft and performing.

• **Walk your family through the audition process.** Many parents think it's simply about coming out to Hollywood and being discovered. Let them know that it's more complicated than what they've seen in the movies. Introduce them to the audition process from start to finish. Tell them about casting notices, agent submissions, callbacks and producer sessions. It will help them understand what you mean when you use words like "SAG," "co-star" or "on avail."

• **Show your family your plan.** Tell them your overall goals and your *career plan* for achieving those goals (from class to mailings to auditioning and so on). This will show them that it's not just a dream, but something tangible that you're serious about. Plus, by giving them a clear career plan, it also will make you more responsible and accountable for your own actions. Once you tell your family your plan, you need to follow through; you have to practice what you preach.

• **Tell your family about your accomplishments.** If you get an agent, an audition or an acting job (no matter how small), tell them. That will show your family that you ARE on a successful path, that you ARE doing more than simply saying, "I'm an actor."

• **Control the message.** There are many ways to communicate with your family about your career. One alternative is a quick, informative e-mail. In an e-mail, you have more control; it allows you to put a more positive spin on whatever you want to tell them. It also minimizes the possibility of being trapped in a conversation you don't want to have. Here's an example of a mock e-mail:

"Hi mom,

Hope everything is going well. I'm thinking of you guys. It's beautiful in L.A. today and I'm feeling really good. I did a scene in class last night that went really well and my acting coach loved it! He says I'm progressing. I can't wait to go back next week. I also met with a potential agent this week and I'm waiting to hear from a few more. Wish me luck. I ALSO have an audition for an independent film coming up this weekend so I'm preparing, keeping busy. Well, I gotta run, but tell dad I said hi and I'll chat with you soon!

Love, Ben

P.S. Oh, tell Aunt Amy I saw George Clooney at the Grove the other day!"

Keep it succinct and most of all...keep it positive. That's not to say you can't share your struggles or feelings with your family. They can be a great sounding board for talking through your problems. However, when it comes to your career, being positive and putting positive energy out to your family will help relieve the pressure.

• **Share success stories.** Tell your family the many stories of struggle and success from accomplished actors. Every successful actor has had to pay their dues. See the end of the book for some great Success Stories to share with your family.

• **Surviving the family holiday.** There's no getting around it: family holidays are stressful for actors. That's when you get the aunts, uncles, grandparents and cousins asking, "How you doing out there, are you on a TV show yet?" It's even more painful when you have those discussions about when you're going to settle down, when you're going to give your mother grandkids, or why you won't go into business with your brother, and so on. Sure it's done out of love, concern or even humor, but it's grating to have to constantly explain yourself.

You'll also face these "what-are-you-doing" questions from your hometown friends who you haven't seen in a while. It can be frustrating to not only explain what you're doing, but also to deal with the constant ribbing ("Oh, it's the big L.A. movie star!").

The solution is...have a plan. Have an idea of what you're going to say to your family and friends so you're not caught off guard when the questions arise. Have a list of what you're going to tell them (what you've been working on, accomplishments, etc.). Once again, keep it honest and keep it positive.

A Reliance On You Being The Point Person

If there's a problem at home, are you the one your parents call? Do you have to settle the arguments between your siblings? Do you have to help your mother get out of a bad mood? Do you have to listen to your father complain about your mother's bad mood? Do you have to help plan family events? Do you talk to your family a few times a day or *more*?

If you do, then you are most certainly the point person in your family, which can be extremely distracting to your career. There is usually one point person that everyone in the family relies on to take care of family issues...and yes, sometimes that point person can be one of the children.

I had a student (Mary) who missed an audition because she was on the phone that morning refereeing a three-way call between her mother and brother. After the two-hour conversation, Mary was so emotionally drained and mentally exhausted that she couldn't focus on her sides. She was too wiped out and so she decided to skip the audition. All she could do was go back to bed.

She made up an excuse to her agent, saying she was sick. Mary felt terrible for doing it, but she at least found solace in the fact that she solved the problem for her mother and brother.

Next week, Mary got the same phone call.

She asked me for my advice. I first reminded her that she wasn't a therapist or family counselor. Then I asked her what would happen if she didn't take the call. Mary said that if she didn't answer the phone and intervene, her mother and brother would either continue to fight or they would resolve the issue themselves. Regardless, they would inevitably be back at it again the next week.

So I asked, "Then who are you really helping?"

She said, "Actually, nobody."

I continued, "And who are you hurting?"

Thinking back to her skipped audition, Mary replied, "Me."

The burden of being the point person

Being the point person isn't easy.

I was the point person in my family. I was the one my family called if they had a problem, if they needed someone to settle an argument, if they were looking for advice, or if they were down and needed a quick pick-me-up.

What's worse, they would call me at work. As a go-getter agent in the '80s, this was horribly distracting. I would get calls at my office at all hours of the day which would deter me from my work. It was mentally and emotionally draining, and my work suffered.

I finally reached a point where I couldn't do it any more. I had to tell my family that they had to solve their own problems with each other; I would no longer mediate. While it caused some friction for a while, once I got my family out of the habit of calling me for everything, I was able to maintain a relationship with them without the pressures or distraction of being the point person.

Taking on the burden of your family issues is nothing more than extra weight. Not only are you enabling your family, you're also sacrificing your own dreams and career goals.

Family issues are too much of a Distraction, and unfortunately they're hard to put aside. Many of you were brought up to "always put family first." That's not a bad philosophy. You do need to be there for your family when they need you most, just as they would hopefully be there for you. However, that doesn't mean you have to absorb *all* of the family drama. Every family has a caretaker and if you want an acting career, that *can't be you!* You will have no time for it.

The point person is often the most responsible in the family. Your family will always look to that person who is good at helping. The problem is, the more you help, the more everyone leans on you and depends on you. Suddenly, you're responsible for helping *everyone*.

Moreover, they think that, as an actor, you have loads of free time. You don't work a normal schedule so they assume that you're *available* to deal with these issues, to help out whenever they need you. It's like you're an on-call, 24/7 family counselor.

Being the point person is a choice

Once again, it comes down to Fear. It's easy to get wrapped up in this role of being the caretaker, especially if that's part of your nature. Solving the family problems can be more familiar and comfortable, especially if you've been doing it your whole life. The longer it continues, the more you will be accustomed to this role and the easier it will be to get lost in it.

This pressure of being the point person isn't limited to just your immediate family -- it also translates to your *family of friends*.

Each family of friends has its own point person, the one friend that is the catalyst holding everyone together, the one that's there as a shoulder to cry on or to plan the next big outing. Once again this is typically the most responsible, practical and organized person in the group. The problem is that this person might start out simply as a helping hand, giving a good piece of advice or solving a problem. Next thing they know, they're the point person.

Chances are, if you're the point person in your immediate family, you're also the point person in your family of friends... which is a double whammy to your acting career.

Whether it's your friends or your family, being the one who's expected to have all the answers can be an unnecessary Distraction. It's best to nip it in the bud sooner rather than later.

Setting boundaries

You have to be willing to step up and tell your family "No" from time to time. You have to summon the strength to tell them that sometimes you're not available, sometimes you're too busy, and sometimes they just need to resolve their own issues.

Trust me, from my own personal experience, I know that's not easy -- especially if you've been the point person your whole life -- but you need to do it. Eventually, they'll understand. They are adults, after all, and part of being an adult is being responsible for one's own self.

You are allowed the freedom to focus on your own life and career...and you need to be willing to take it. In order to set boundaries with your family, you have to become a little selfish, especially with your time. After all, you need that time (and energy) to put into your acting work. Here are some pointers to help you establish boundaries with your family:

• **Let it go to voice mail.** You have to remember that you don't *always* have to answer that phone call from mom or dad, or immediately return that message from your brother or sister, or text message back to your best friend. You have the right to turn your phone off or just...let it go to voice mail.

• **Set scheduled times to chat.** Find times in your week that are convenient for you and set weekly or bi-weekly phone calls. Even though you're not working a 9-to-5 job, you should still be setting up a work schedule or routine for yourself. Make your phone call to your family part of that schedule. This will help you be more accountable and responsible with both your family and your own acting time. That way you can avoid being interrupted, and give your family your full attention when you do have time to talk.

• **Take advantage of e-mail.** It's shorter, sweeter, and you can get to the point quicker. If you have a family that needs "daily updates," shoot them an e-mail.

• **Explain your life as an actor.** Once again, communicate. Let them know what the daily life of an actor in Hollywood involves and how busy you are (or should be). Show them why you might not be available all the time.

• **Tell your family that you can't be the point person.** Let them know that while they're important to you, you simply can't be there to solve every single problem. Let them know that you want to help, but you can't be the family mediator, counselor or planner *all the time.* Just to warn you, they might be upset with you at first, but if they love you (and I'm sure they do), they will ultimately understand that you need your own time and space for your own career. In fact, over time, they will grow to respect you for taking charge of your life and doing what you need to do to become successful.

RELATIONSHIPS

Starting, building and maintaining a romantic **relationship** is always at least a bit of a challenge...especially if you're an actor whose first priority is their career.

There are many successful actors that are involved in long-term, healthy, stable, giving relationships. A relationship with the right person can bring a lot of joy, excitement, growth and most of all comfort to your life. There is nothing better than sharing your journey with someone who loves you as much as you love them.

The nature of a career in Hollywood, however, offers many challenges to a relationship, especially when it comes to such vital necessities as time, energy and dedication.

An acting career can put a strain on any kind of relationship, especially if your partner isn't an actor and doesn't understand the work involved. Having an acting career means constant hard work, inconsistent pay and unrelenting devotion. Pursuing an acting career requires a tremendous amount of patience from your partner.

When you don't have that, your relationship can become a Distraction to your career.

An unhealthy relationship

All relationships do require some work. Some believe that if you love each other enough, it shouldn't be work. I define working at your relationship as a mutual exploration to understand and help fulfill each other's needs and desires. That type of work can lead you to a strong bond, a healthy partnership.

In an *unhealthy* relationship, that work can sometimes lead us to give in, give up or sacrifice our own *individual* needs and desires. We relent to the pressures of the relationship and the expectations of our partners -- distracting us from what we really want to do.

I have seen many actors struggle with girlfriend issues or boyfriend issues, and even spousal issues. Sure, every relationship has its problems, but when these problems outweigh the good times, they become a Distraction. Because these significant others are so important, these problems are tough to shake or simply ignore. They fester in your mind and heart and they distract you from the work at hand. You love that person and you want to fix the problem within the relationship, so that's where you put all your focus.

Relationships are similar to family in that way. Your partner will have a tremendous influence over anything and everything that you do. They will impact you and your decisions on a daily basis. They may put certain pressures or restraints on you (consciously or unconsciously) if they feel your career is becoming more of a priority than the relationship.

It can become more problematic when your partner isn't involved in an artistic field. Just like your family, they might not understand why you chose this unpredictable profession. If they have a steady job, they won't understand when money is tight or why you have to work at night or how you might have to leave to work an acting job. They don't understand your true desire and need to pursue this career. Or they do understand it, but don't really accept it. At heart, they don't support your decision to be an actor. They might *say* that they support you, but their actions say otherwise.

This unhealthy relationship will affect you, going beyond just the discussions and arguments over your career and your priorities. When you don't have someone who understands or supports your dreams, your Confidence level sinks, making you question yourself.

It keeps you from putting your energy toward your craft and career. You love and respect this person so much and to have them not support you is depressing. It trickles down into everything that you do.

It's even more difficult when you're married or if your boyfriend or girlfriend has moved out to Los Angeles with you. Suddenly, there is that extra pressure on you to produce. If you're married, you may need to provide for your spouse (and children). That can be tough with an acting career, especially when you're just starting out. If you've had a loved one move out with you, there will be a feeling of responsibility toward them. You'll feel like you need to show them why it was the right move to make. All that does is add to the stress.

They just don't understand

The most common Distraction I've seen in relationships is the metaphorical tug-of-war with the actor and his or her career. In many relationships, the partner expects the relationship to be the first priority. If an acting career is important to you, though, then that acting career must be the first priority.

Your significant other will want your time and energy. That doesn't mean they're bad partners -- it's only natural. If they don't understand why you can't always give them that time and energy, problems can arise.

I've seen actors come to class moody, distant and agitated, sometimes with tears in their eyes, because they just had a fight with their girlfriend or boyfriend. It's almost always about their acting career taking priority over the relationship. The most common thing I hear is, "They just don't understand."

Many actors get distracted with the pressure to be the *good* boyfriend or girlfriend. They do whatever they can to appease their partner, including forfeiting everything they came out to Los Angeles to accomplish. They play the role of the obedient girlfriend or boyfriend, slowly but surely losing themselves in the relationship.

Or they become the point person in the relationship -- the responsible, practical, organized one who has to take care of all their partner's needs. Once again, all their efforts go into the relationship and there is nothing left to put toward a career.

Sometimes this relationship Distraction is a little tougher to see. You can get so wrapped up in keeping your partner happy that you are blind to how much you're sacrificing in your career. Then suddenly, months and even years have gone by and you have nothing in your own life or career to show for it.

It's easier to spot when the person blatantly tells you they're not supportive. Unfortunately, I've seen just as much of a Distraction from actors who say they have partners who "totally understand and support them." When push comes to shove…they don't.

I should have gotten on that plane

Jenny was a beautiful, young actress I represented in New York. She had a gradual, steady build in her career with commercials, co-stars and guest stars. As her star continued to rise, I got Jenny an audition for a series regular on a hit TV show that filmed in Los Angeles. It also happened to be her favorite show.

She was very excited, but I was concerned. I got to know Jenny quite well. She had an out-of-work boyfriend named Bobby who was jealous of her career. He constantly seemed to try and talk her out of opportunities, sabotaging her career at every turn. Plus, he was very controlling. Needless to say, Bobby and I did not get along. Jenny loved him, though, and assured me that he *was* supportive of her career. I knew better.

Jenny went on the audition in New York and the next day I got a call from the casting director. They wanted to fly her to L.A. for a screen test. The casting director told me that Jenny was perfect for the role and the only one being considered. This was Jenny's big moment. She was excited, ready and prepared to take advantage of the opportunity.

Bobby didn't want her to go. He gave Jenny reasons why she shouldn't screen test: she could find just as many acting jobs in New York, this is where their family and friends were and New York was their home. They argued and Jenny almost backed out until she realized the significance of this career opportunity.

I put Jenny in a cab and off she went to JFK International Airport to screen-test for the TV show. An hour later, I got a phone call from Jenny saying that she decided *not* to get on the plane. She told me that I should cancel her screen test because she wasn't going to move to Los Angeles. I was stunned and asked her why.

Here's roughly what she said:

"Oh my God, Scott, it was like a movie. Just as I was about to step on the plane, I hear someone yelling out my name. I turned around and I see Bobby running down the terminal with flowers in his hand. It was the sweetest thing. He got on one knee and in front of everyone, Bobby proposed to me. Scott…I'm getting married!"

Oy!

Jenny never got on that plane. She never screen-tested. She never appeared on her favorite show. She *did* end up marrying Bobby…and after two rocky, tumultuous years playing the role of "depressed wife" and not doing anything toward her career, she divorced him.

Lucky for her, Jenny was able to jump back in the game and ultimately rebound. A few years after her divorce, Jenny got a role as a series regular on a hit TV show…that shot in L.A. Jenny continues to be a successful working actress.

Recently, I bumped into Jenny at an awards dinner. After we chatted for a while, she chuckled and said, "I should have gotten on that plane." I gave her a hug and as I was leaving, she called out, "Tell your students to 'get on that plane.' Tell them my story...just change my name!"

Distractions don't always smack you in the face. They're not always noticeable right away; but if you're in an unhealthy relationship, they *will* at some point rear their ugly head.

Relationships are familiar

As easy as it would be to put the blame on your significant other for distracting you from your career, you can't. Just like with family, it comes down to *you* and your personal choice.

Whether it's blatant or more subtle, your relationship can only be a Distraction if you choose to let it be. After all, you have the power to work on your relationship; you have the power to change the relationship. You have the power to set boundaries, find balance and have a healthy relationship.

However, many actors choose to let an unhealthy relationship become a Distraction to their career...and the main reason why, as always, is Fear.

Working toward a relationship, even an unhealthy, unstable one, is often more familiar and more comfortable than entering into the unknown territory of an acting career.

Many of us play a similar role in our relationships as we do in our family. If you're the point person in your family, chances are you're the point person in your relationship. If you're more dependent on your family, you probably expect the same from your partner. If you felt abandoned by your family or if you were left on your own, you might either be very independent or very insecure in your relationship. We can identify with these particular roles and responsibilities and we seek solace in their predictability.

When we take on these roles in relationships, they can become very comforting and familiar. Having a relationship can provide a wonderful escape from your acting career. Whether it's going out to dinner, cuddling on the couch, making love, talking, and yes, even working on your relationship, it's a welcome reprieve from your career. It feels better for the moment and it's easy to get wrapped up in that feeling.

I'm not saying that's a bad thing, but you can't do it all the time. If acting is important to you, then your acting career must be your first priority. That doesn't mean you can't have a relationship as well. You simply need to find a balance.

Finding balance

Okay, after reading all of this, many of you are probably terrified of having a relationship while you pursue an acting career. Don't be; it can be done. Here are a few simple tips to help you maintain balance in your relationship and to ensure that your relationship doesn't become a Distraction to your career.

• **Be up** front **about your Want.** This way you're not presenting any false impressions of yourself to prospective partners. Know what your priorities are and share them with your partner. Tell them how focused, determined and passionate you are about being an actor. Then, you also need to acknowledge, respect and embrace your partner's goals, dreams and ambitions as well.

• **Talk about your life as an actor.** Much like you did with your family, communicate to your partner about the time, commitment and sacrifices that an acting career requires so they know what to expect. Also, learn to be a good listener. To be a good actor, you need to be a good listener. The same is true in a healthy relationship.

• **Be with someone who's supportive.** It's important that you have a relationship with someone compatible, someone who "gets" you and what you're doing. Make sure you're with someone who is loving, compassionate, understanding and for God's sake, not someone who is needy! Your acting career is needy enough. Remember though, that support is a two-way street. If you want your partner to encourage you in your pursuit, then you must encourage them in their pursuit.

• **Set boundaries.** As I said, it's easy for you to get lost in the comfort of your relationship. Be aware of it. Make sure that while you make time for your partner, you also make time for your career work. Sit down with your partner and discuss each other's career needs.

You need to let them know that you will need time and space -- physical and emotional -- to put toward your career. You have to also respect that they will need time and space for their own career as well. Make rules and try to stick by them.

As with most things, relationships come down to communication and commitment. I truly believe that when two people love each other, they want to help fulfill each other's destiny. Find the person that brings out the best in you, not the worst in you. Find someone who loves you for who you really are. Always be open and honest in your relationship and help each other grow as individuals, free of Distractions.

OVER-EXTENDING

There are those actors that do find a balance when it comes to their survival job(s), family and relationships. They have the support, understanding and most of all, time to tackle their goals, both in their career and their personal life.

Many of those actors struggle with a different kind of balancing act, juggling many goals. Many actors simply try taking on too much, and that **over-extending** can be a Distraction.

With high hopes and stars in their eyes, these actors think they can *do it all*. They want to be a jack-of-all-trades: acting, writing, directing, producing, sound design, you name it.

Then there are those that over-extend when it comes to their hobbies, community work or other skills and trades (teaching, graphic design, building websites, decorating, planning, massage, consulting, etc.).

These actors have *way* too many things on their plate and they struggle to multitask and get everything done at once. As I've said throughout this book, I'm a big believer in working hard and setting goals. I believe that dedicated, hard-working individuals can accomplish multiple tasks. I believe you can do anything and all that you want...but not *all at once*. You need to take one thing at a time. Once you become a successful actor, then you can become the painter, writer, director or rock star you always wanted to be.

You have the choice to avoid Distractions. You can do it. You need to prioritize and simplify your life. Focus on what's most important -- your acting career -- and make and take the time for it. Don't get caught up in those things that can sidetrack you from what you came out to Hollywood to do...act!

CHAPTER 2
ADDICTIONS

As you hit roadblocks in your journey to becoming a successful actor in Hollywood, you will often find yourself looking to emotionally, physically and mentally escape. Because actors face rejection and disappointment on a regular basis, it's not surprising how many turn to various **Addictions**, such as alcohol, drugs, smoking, food and even sex.

Addictions are the most dangerous of the Three Steps to Failure because they will not only harm your career, but also your life.

Simply put, an Addiction is the desire to continually partake in an activity despite knowing that there will be harmful consequences. It's doing something you know...*you shouldn't be doing.* Addictions are mood-altering activities a person takes to help them escape. An addict justifies their actions (their Addiction) with the thought that it will help them deal with a problem or an emotion, like anger, depression, stress and Fear.

Drinking, eating and even consuming caffeine...they are all ways we deal with stress. None of them are necessarily bad...as long as you limit your intake. It's when you become *dependent* on those influences, or you take on harmful influences like drugs, that they become a problem. They become Addictions.

Every generation in Hollywood has had its "party scene." It's part of the allure of being a young actor. It's a communal scene where actors meet new people, celebrate their youth and newfound independence, and share their hopes, desires and dreams.

As inviting as the party scene can be, it can also open the door to temptation. That presents a challenge to new actors who will inevitably look for vices, ways to relieve their frustrations and Fear in both their career and their life in the new city. Whether it's drinking, drug use or even smoking, it can start as an experiment, then turn into an "occasional thing," then a habit and next thing you know…it's an Addiction.

That Addiction then becomes a major Obstacle, slowly chipping away at your Talent, self-esteem, hope and purpose.

WHERE DO ADDICTIONS COME FROM?

The topic of Addictions is a very complex and controversial one. Most experts agree that Addiction is a brain disease of sorts, a result of chemicals and neurotransmitters in the brain being out of balance. It's a mix up in the brain that tells a person that even though they recognize that doing this activity is wrong, they still need to do it.

As far as what exactly triggers Addictions, that gets a little more complicated. Many people say that stress is the number one cause of Addiction, as the brain and the body constantly search for ways to relieve tension. Many say that hormones play a role as well as hereditary genes. If you have a history of Addiction in your family, there is a strong probability that you will be more susceptible.

Still others associate Addictions with societal influences. Some will take on Addictions to fit in with certain groups or because it's part of their culture and environment. Or they will simply take on these Addictions as a source of entertainment, something they associate with having a good time, and that slowly develops into a dependency.

I am not an expert on Addiction. My intent in this chapter is not to solve any Addiction problem you might have…you need counseling, a 12-step program, rehab or treatment for that. Rather, I want to help you identify the types of Addictions that I've seen many actors experience. I want to shed some light on where those Addictions originate, how they can hurt you and your career, and how you can get past them.

Why actors face Addictions

A life as an actor in Hollywood can be an emotional roller coaster. There will be some incredible highs and a TON of lows…and it's those lows that tend to lead actors to look for something to make them feel better. Whether it's a coping mechanism, a comforting crutch or just the need to feel *high*, actors will turn to negative outside influences.

For an actor pursuing an acting career in Hollywood, many of these Addictions come from Fear. Addictions emerge from the struggles actors face in their careers. You will feel disappointed, rejected, depressed, etc. You will sometimes question your acting dream, your purpose, your future. Your self-esteem will plummet and you will ask, "Why am I doing this to myself?!" Or worse, "Was my father right?!"

Creative people (actors, singers, painters, writers) are inherently more sensitive and emotional than others. They are usually more aware, more in touch with their feelings. Actors, specifically, are trained to draw from their emotions and to experience whatever is happening around them, moment to moment. Combine that sensitivity with a volatile career like acting, and it becomes easier for Fear to creep in. Actors turn to Addictions to numb themselves from negative experiences, to avoid that Fear, .

That applies to both the Fear of Failure and the Fear of Success.

Making a habit out of drinking, over-eating, not eating enough or doing drugs are ways an actor deals with their Fear of Failure. They take on these Addictions because they feel like they're not good enough, they're letting themselves down, letting others down, and sacrificing other opportunities.

Those actors with a Fear of Success turn to Addictions when they start to experience their life *changing*. They find vices when they have to branch out of their Comfort Zone, when they have to deal with the limelight, higher expectations, and the new pressures of success.

I'm not naïve. I know that many of you will drink or smoke or do drugs at some point. For those of you who occasionally take part in these activities, it doesn't mean you have an Addiction or that you will ever be addicted. However, you do need to be aware of where these desires come from. You need to look at your own life and figure out how often you turn to these negative influences and more importantly, WHY!

I will help you identify and confront the most common Addictions that actors face, the most common ways that Addiction can self-sabotage an actor's career.

ALCOHOL

Many people drink or at least try **alcohol** at some point in their lives. In the life of an actor, it might seem almost unavoidable.

Whether it's at parties, industry functions, hanging out with other actors after class, a show, a film shoot, whatever, the "let's-go-grab-a-drink" mentality has always been part of the acting scene.

Sometimes that's okay. We all need to unwind, decompress or celebrate an accomplishment, but from these "social occasions," alcoholism *can* creep in.

Alcoholism is a disease that you can willingly trigger and enable. At its core, alcoholism is continuing to drink even when you're drinking causes problems (health, behavioral, social, career) to you as well as others. Many people that are addicted to alcohol are often aware of their Addiction, but they still can't stop. Or worse, they are in full denial of their drinking problem.

Alcohol is a depressant, and in an industry fraught with rejection, you don't need an external depressant. I've seen how alcoholism derails careers. As you work hard for that one big opportunity, you don't want an alcohol Addiction to get in the way.

She was supposed to be a star!

I had a student whom I'll call Lucy. She already had some acting training before we met. She was 20 years old and everyone who met her instantly knew that she was going to be a successful actress. When they saw her act, they knew she would be a star.

She was not "model beautiful," but she had something extraordinary about her...big blue eyes, coquettish smile and an infectious personality. She was charming, funny and endearing with just enough "quirk" that everybody wanted to be her friend.

I introduced her to an agent and he immediately signed her. Soon, she was off auditioning and booking commercials and co-star roles on TV shows. For a survival job, Lucy worked as a hostess in a restaurant (a perfect job for her personality).

Every night after work, Lucy would sit at the bar, have a nightcap and entertain everyone. Soon, her nightcap became a few drinks, and then it became *too many* drinks. Each morning, she would get up for her auditions hungover, foggy and unfocused. No matter how much Visine she used, her eyes were still bloodshot, and her pocket strips of Listerine couldn't hide the smell of last night's alcohol on her breath.

After an audition for a TV show, her agent received a call from the casting director saying that Lucy came in "obviously hungover." They wanted to hire her, but they were fearful that she had a drinking problem. A former alcohol addict himself, Lucy's agent confronted her on her problem and, at first, she denied it.

However, after she saw how it was affecting her career, she agreed to seek help. Lucy joined a 12-step program and is sober now. She is back at her acting and still has the potential to hit it big. Still...this Addiction took three years off of her career.

To drink or not to drink

To make drinking a part of your life is an individual choice. With that comes a responsibility and accountability to yourself and to others. But there are times you should *never* drink; more specifically, when it could interfere with your acting work.

You should never drink before a class, an audition or a job. You should never drink *the night* before a class, an audition or a job. Also, you should never, ever drink and drive.

If you choose to drink, you need to monitor yourself, especially the reasons *why* you are drinking. Drinking to cope with pain, frustration, depression, anger or any other negative emotion is detrimental to your well-being.

Having a beer to celebrate booking a commercial is great.... congratulations! Having a six pack of beer the night before you shoot the commercial is a problem.

There are several red flags for someone who has a drinking problem and a potential for an alcohol Addiction. These are the warning signs that you can watch out for in both yourself and friends.

Alcohol Red Flags

• **Impaired conditions:** Slurred speech, stumbling, disorientation or a lack of coordination; displaying "drunken behavior" regularly.

• **Erratic behavior:** Shifting from happiness and giddiness to depression, impatience and even anger at the drop of a hat.

• **Self-neglect:** Not caring about appearance and health; poor hygiene, unkempt and disheveled. Red, inflamed eyes, a swollen or blotchy face.

• **Hangover syndrome:** Sluggish, groggy, tired from dehydration, sometimes nauseous; smelling of alcohol.

DRUGS

A drug Addiction is one of the easiest (and most damaging) Addictions to fall into.

Drugs can give you a high, a sense of power, a feeling of invincibility and omnipotence. They create a false sense of hope, security and Confidence -- that you can do anything or be anyone. It can make you think that you have "super powers." It's narcissism at an extreme level.

Drugs are also used to numb the pain. People turn to drugs as a buffer between their feelings and the world around them. They numb the user to the point that they fall out of touch with their feelings and feel nothing but the effects of the drug.

Not every actor who comes to L.A. does drugs, but each and every one of them will at some point in their career face the temptation. Each generation has its illegal substances, its wild, responsibility-free, "nothing-matters-but-this-moment" lifestyle -- whether it's the 1920s Hollywood Prohibition Era, the Reefer Madness of the '30s, the psychedelic drug movement of the '60s, the Coked-Out '80s, Ecstacy of the '90s or prescription drug abuse today.

A Drug Addiction is always easy to get trapped in.

I'm going to be the next Brad Pitt!

I received an e-mail from an 18-year-old kid from Missouri, who had seen me on my TV show *Fight For Fame.* I'll call him Cal. Cal wanted to come to Los Angeles, study with me and pursue an acting career. He wrote that he was going to get his finances together and he would be out in L.A. in six months.

Sure enough, six months later, Cal showed up at my studio ready to begin his acting career. He was a handsome, blond-haired, blue-eyed, determined young man. He had some acting experience in his hometown, but he was here to train and focus on his Hollywood dreams. Cal said with great self-assurance, "I'm going to be the next Brad Pitt!" I believed him. He got into class right away and studied intensely. He was eager to learn, a hardworker and he had a positive outlook.

As opportunity would have it, one day a photographer stopped him outside my studio and told him, "You have a great look." He called him in for a national print job and Cal booked it. That gave Cal even more motivation to work harder and, as such, he progressed quickly.

However, a few months later, Cal began to show up to class late and unprepared for his assignments. He also came in looking run-down and tired. I finally pulled him aside and asked him what was going on.

Cal said he had been out "partying" at the clubs with all these new friends from his modeling shoot. I could tell from talking with him that while he was enjoying the attention, he was also overwhelmed by the scene. I discovered that Cal was using cocaine…and his cocaine use became a big problem.

Cal started to miss class altogether. He wouldn't return my phone calls. I found out later that Cal was arrested for a DUI and the police found cocaine in his car. After only being in Los Angeles for a year, everything he worked for started to unravel. As most drug users eventually do, he hit rock bottom. His parents came to get him and took him back home to Missouri. Recently, I received an e-mail from Cal saying he was now drug-free and hoping to return to Hollywood…still with dreams of being the next Brad Pitt.

Just like alcohol, many actors will experiment with a drug of some kind or another in their lifetime. I can tell you not to do it, but I know better. So instead, I'll tell you to BE CAREFUL. As you can see from Cal's story, drug use is a slippery slope with horrible consequences.

Drug Red Flags

• **Extreme behavior:** Cocaine and other stimulants make the user excitable, hyper, restless, anxious, unable to focus; can become excessively manic, jumpy or "twitchy." Marijuana users display sluggish behavior, paranoia or unusual giddiness.

• **Mental affects:** Regular drug users often get confused easily, are more apt to be forgetful, or worse, they have completely illogical thinking.

• **Looking and acting tired:** Some who smoke pot generally have a tired, drawn look with red, puffy, inflamed eyes. Harder drugs like cocaine lead to wide eyes, dilated pupils, as well as a red nose or inflamed nostrils with too much use. Sleep deprivation, dehydration and constant "highs" and "lows" can damage the body and mind.

• **Talkative:** Drug users tend to talk excessively; overly intent on the subject at hand, what's important to them at that moment. They are more likely to say inappropriate things.

Alcohol And Drug Treatment

If you have a drinking or drug problem, you need professional help. You can't kick it on your own. You need a place to detox, a 12-step treatment program, counselors and a support group that will help you get past the Addiction. On top of that, there are some things you can do individually to help you stay clean after you've kicked the habit.

• **Keep up with your 12-step program.** It's always good to be surrounded by others who are struggling with their own Addictions and can understand what you're going through. Not only will you gain some insight from listening to their stories, but you will also get advice for how to cope with your Addiction.

• **Be open and honest with friends and family.** When you're seeking treatment, don't be afraid or ashamed to tell your close friends and family about your Addiction. They can be there for you to lean on. Be open with your friends so they know why you're not drinking or partying.

• **Avoid functions where there might be drugs or alcohol involved.** Addicts who have cleaned up say the temptation is always still present in their lives. Try to avoid that temptation at all costs.

• **Find other positive outlets.** Find substitutions that can replace that high you get from drugs or alcohol. Running, lifting weights, aerobics, yoga, meditation, gardening, cooking, golf, tennis, movies…find something that will keep you occupied and satisfied with your life. Focusing your energy and working on your career will not only keep you from drinking and doing drugs, but will also lead you to a positive outcome…success!

EATING DISORDERS

There are many actors who deal with **eating disorders**. There are several different kinds, but the three most common are:

Bulimia
Anorexia
Binge-eating

Bulimia and anorexia stem almost exclusively from image issues, while binge-eating is more of an anxiety-related Addiction. It's an escape from the pressures of life, much like drugs and alcohol.

Eating disorders are just as deadly of a disease as any other kind of Addiction. They come from a number of places…family history, genes, upbringing, societal expectations, low self-esteem, industry pressure and worst of all, Fear.

Hollywood will have certain physical expectations for actors, and you need to come to terms with that. It will be up to you to monitor yourself, to ensure that the desire to drop or gain a few pounds doesn't become a problem. Sometimes that can be tough in an image-conscious, weight-obsessed town like L.A., where you will be bombarded by what Hollywood considers "beauty."

If you're leading man material or an ingénue, you know that you have to be in good shape. There are many talented actors in Los Angeles, including several that fit your same type. Often times, casting will come down to appearance, who looks better, who fits the mold of what's hot on TV now. I'm not saying that it's right; I'm just telling you that's how it is.

For women, the struggle comes with the perceived need to be thin. Unfortunately, this business celebrates the skinny, the size zero. The industry ideal of beauty is often defined by models and starlets that are much skinnier than the average woman. Often, female actresses feel the need to lose weight at any cost, just to keep up.

It can affect men as well. I've seen many leading men not get roles because casting directors said they were "a little too heavy," they're "full in the face" or they "have a gut." At the same time, they're often not *heavy enough* to get character roles. They're stuck in between and looking for a change, looking to lose or gain.

You need to know your type and be comfortable with your type…as long as it *doesn't jeopardize your health*. For example, if you want to be an ingénue and you think you would be better served by losing a few pounds…by all means order that salad. If you're a character actor and a couple of extra pounds will help you get work, find a healthy way to maintain that weight.

As I've said throughout this book, your best chance at getting work is for you to feel confident in who you are…and that includes your appearance. When it comes to your health, though, especially your eating habits, you need to watch yourself closely.

She looked a little heavy on camera

I had an actress in my class whom I'll call Amanda. She was a young, All-American type from the Midwest. She was very talented and hardworking, and on the surface, she appeared to have a lot of Confidence.

She quickly got representation, started booking small jobs and got a nice break as a guest star on a hit show as the lead character's girlfriend.

After Amanda appeared on the show, her agent told her that "she looked a little heavy on camera." He suggested that she lose a little weight and tone up, especially around the "lower half of her body."

Amanda smiled and told her agent, "No problem." When she got back home, she broke down crying. She was upset by what her agent told her, but she knew that eating was always a problem for her. She was very sensitive about her weight. When the agent offered his suggestion, Amanda knew he was right, and she didn't want to risk the possibility of losing work (there was talk of her role on the show becoming a recurring guest star).

Because of her love of eating, Amanda didn't know how she would lose the weight. A couple days later, she was at a birthday party, still feeling depressed about her weight situation. Even though she vowed she wouldn't eat any birthday cake, she gave into her temptation and had a slice…and then another…and then another. Amanda felt so sick to her stomach that she went into the bathroom and forced herself to throw up, something she had never done before.

Amanda told me that the minute she threw up, she felt "a euphoric sense of satisfaction and relief." It was at that moment that she realized how she was going to control her weight. Amanda secretly began binging and purging. She would eat and eat and eat, including tons of sweets, and then force herself to throw up…and she would do this up to six times a day!

Friends started to notice that she wasn't looking well, but nobody would have guessed the cause. The irony, she said, was that she did this to have control over her weight, but it was her eating disorder that had control over her.

One day, Amanda finally took a good look at her daily habits and realized that she needed to seek help. She still struggles every day, but she's in control of her eating disorder now and she's continuing her career as a working actress.

Bulimia And Anorexia

Bulimia and anorexia are two distinct eating disorders, but they both share one important trait: they both come from an uncontrollable desire to lose weight and to keep losing weight beyond healthy limits.

Bulimia is a disorder that includes eating large quantities of food, often several times a day and then immediately purging the food, mainly through vomiting. Again, this comes down to "control" as well as feelings of guilt or shame. Bulimics (like Amanda) will often eat unhealthy foods, feel guilty and then purge, making them feel empty once again. So they eat again…and this unhealthy cycle continues.

Anorexia is defined as having abnormally low weight with the fear of gaining weight. It's a deadly disease because people who are anorexic often willingly omit the essential vitamins and nutrients that food provides, making them sick.

According to the American Psychiatric Association, anorexics and bulimics are often perfectionists: people who are very driven and like to be in control. When their lives start to spiral out of control, they often turn to their weight or diet as that is something they *can* control. It becomes an obsession or an Addiction.

Bulimia and Anorexia Red Flags

• **Weight loss:** A problem occurs when weight loss is happening at a rapid pace, to the point where the person begins to look unhealthy and continues to lose weight.

• **Talking about body image:** An obsession with image; weight becomes their main topic of conversation, whether its calorie intake, diets or different techniques to keep weight off.

• **Not ordering food:** This can range from ordering only small portions to not eating at all. Anorexics will often make excuses for not eating, such as "Oh, I ate earlier." On the flip side, bulimics will often order a huge portion of food when dining out, but will almost always visit the bathroom immediately after eating, often multiple times.

• **Taking steps to stop weight gain:** Working out excessively, taking supplements or weight loss pills, using laxatives, enemas or simply fasting.

Tearing into a bunch of cheeseburgers

I introduced one of my students, whom I'll call Eddie, to a sitcom casting director. He was a funny, pudgy character actor with an endearing, teddy bear charm.

The casting director loved Eddie and she promised to bring him in for her show...and she did. Although he didn't land the part, she kept his headshot on file and was determined to find him the "perfect role." A few months later, that role came up. This time, she called Eddie back in to meet directly with the show's producer.

When the casting director saw Eddie again, she was surprised. He had gained quite a bit of weight. He was no longer pudgy, he was now *heavy*...too heavy to cast him in that particular role. Later, she told me that she was really disappointed because she wanted to work with him. After that conversation, I thought it was important to talk to Eddie about his weight gain.

He said that he had been through a lot lately with family and work problems. He told me that when he felt stressed out, he would deal with it by "tearing into a bunch of cheeseburgers." Most people with a binge-eating disorder have a "trigger food." Eddie's was cheeseburgers, which, unfortunately, put on the pounds quickly.

We chatted a bit and the conversation went well. I felt sympathetic for him; you could tell he was ashamed and embarrassed. I recommended he get help and he said he would. Therapy led him to Overeaters Anonymous and, though Eddie still struggles with his weight, he works hard to keep it in check. A few months later, the casting director called him in again and he was back to his pudgy, endearing teddy bear self...and he booked the job.

Binge-eating

We all binge from time to time. We all stuff ourselves, especially if we're having a bad day or if we just want to indulge...or if it's Thanksgiving. The difference is that someone with a **binge-eating** disorder will do it *all the time*, often to deal with feelings of stress, sadness, anger and depression.

They will eat large amounts of food very quickly in the hopes that it will fill that void and make them feel better. They will often binge in private, ashamed of their habits, trying to hide them.

Binge-eating Red Flags

• **Noticeable weight gain:** A sudden increase in weight, going up a few sizes over a short period of time (weeks, months).

• **Depression:** Often leads to binge-eating. The two work hand in hand: if depressed, frustrated or embarrassed, those afflicted will eat to comfort themselves.

• **Unkempt appearance:** Tend to look slovenly and unkempt, from hair to hygiene to clothes. They usually wear the same clothes because that's what fits.

• **Eating unhealthy foods:** Fast food, salty snacks, sweets, soft drinks, etc....these all are part of a binge-eater's diet. There is often a trigger food, one that makes them feel the most comfortable (and is usually the worst for them).

Eating Disorders Treatment

As with any Addiction, if you have an eating disorder -- anorexia, bulimia or binge-eating -- you need to seek therapy, counseling and a treatment program. Here are some other tips that can help you avoid or confront this specific Addiction.

• **Monitor your diet.** Watch what you eat. Make sure you're eating enough healthy foods. Don't ever be afraid to ask friends for help. Also, don't be afraid to hire a nutritionist.

• **Work out regularly.** This will help you keep your weight at a manageable level. If you're fighting anorexia or bulimia, working out regularly (without doing it excessively) can help give you a sense of accomplishment and a good feeling about your body image. I suggest you hire a trainer. There are several nutritionists and trainers in L.A. who are struggling like you to jump-start their careers, and they are often willing to offer deals and discounts to attract new clients.

• **Watch out for triggers.** Acknowledge your trigger food, what you eat when you're feeling depressed, rejected, frustrated, etc.

• **Keep yourself busy with positive activities.** The best would be career work. Read over the Perseverance chapter again. Do what you need to do to stay positive. Remind yourself of your Confidence Affirmations.

OTHER ADDICTIONS

Alcohol, drugs, eating disorders…these are by no means all of the Addictions that actors face and fight in Hollywood, but they are the most common. Nevertheless, an Addiction can be any kind of activity that becomes an obsession, causes harm and disrupts a person's career and life.

One of the most common is smoking. Beyond the obvious health risks, smoking also ages you and damages your appearance, putting lines in your face and yellowing your teeth. It also makes a bad first impression. There is nothing worse than an actor smoking a cigarette right before they walk into an audition. The casting director's first impression is "you smell" and "I want you out of this room as soon as possible."

I've also seen actors with financial Addictions, like gambling and shopping. They'll drain their account to the point that they simply don't have the funds to pursue an acting career…and what a waste *that* is.

I've seen others addicted to their computers and the Internet, especially with sites like MySpace, YouTube, Facebook and a slew of online pornography. The same holds true for video game addicts. Sure, it's nice to have an occasional diversion, but it's sometimes too easy to get lost in these activities, spending hours in front of a TV or computer instead of working on your career.

There will even be those that will be more physical, like a sex Addiction. Besides the possibility of health risks (if having sex with multiple partners), there is an emotional toll that a sex Addiction can take.

Then of course, there are the Addictions like sugar and caffeine. They can't necessarily derail your career, but they can affect your health, so you need to limit your intake or stop altogether.

As I said, it will be easy to get wrapped up in Addictions. There are plenty of temptations and opportunities to avoid facing your career in Hollywood, whether you have a Fear of Failure or a Fear of Success. You have to remind yourself that they are all Distractions -- unhealthy substitutes, roadblocks and Obstacles keeping you from doing what you came to Hollywood to accomplish.

You need to keep a close eye on your activities. Ask yourself what you are trying to escape from. As you uncover these feelings, integrate them into your experience, and turn them into more positive feelings, your need for an Addiction will abate and your joy in the process will increase.

RESOURCES

Alcoholics Anonymous
(323) 936-4343 (L.A. branch)
(800) 923-8722 (hotline)
alcoholics-anonymous.org

Al-Anon
(888) 425-2666
al-anon.org

Narcotics Anonymous
(818) 773-9999
na.org

Marijuana Anonymous
(800) 766-6779
marijuana-anonymous.org

Cocaine Anonymous
(310) 559-5833
ca.org

Overeaters Anonymous
(505) 891-2664
oa.org

Eating Disorders Anonymous
(605) 990-0300
eatingdisordersanonymous.org

Nicotine Anonymous
(415) 750-0328
nicotine-anonymous.org

The Actors' Fund
(800) 221-7303
actorsfund.org

CHAPTER 3
WRONG ACTIONS

Of the Three Steps to Failure, **Wrong Actions** will have the most immediate and profound effect on you and your career. Wrong Actions are the number one way to not only sidetrack you from your career, but also to derail it permanently.

On your way to becoming a successful actor, you will face many choices, decisions that will impact where and how your career will progress. These are decisions that will emerge each and every day. How you respond and what you choose will determine your fate as an actor. You will have the chance to take Right Actions, which will guide you to some wonderful opportunities and eventually to your overall destination...a career in Hollywood.

You will also have the chance to take Wrong Actions, which do nothing but hurt you, your reputation and your career. Although we learn from our mistakes and failures, once you start taking Wrong Actions, a trend begins to develop. You start to form bad habits and those habits affect everything you do.

If you consistently show up late to acting class, you could develop a reputation as irresponsible and uncommitted. If you conduct yourself poorly in an agent meeting, you'll discourage them from wanting to represent you. If you show up unprepared to an audition, you could hurt your chance at a role. If you procrastinate from doing your career work, you will delay your journey to making it in Hollywood.

It will be up to you and you alone to identify these Wrong Actions and ultimately avoid taking them. If you do take them, you must quickly learn from your mistake and turn that Wrong Action into a Right Action.

Wrong Actions come from Fear

As with all Obstacles, actors take Wrong Actions out of Fear, both the Fear of Success and Fear of Failure.

In the Fear chapter, I talked about a student (Tom) who showed up unprepared for my acting class. He told me he was "just lazy," and I told him he was fearful. Tom chose to take the Wrong Action to put off his work because it was easier. He was faced with a choice and he decided not to work on his scene, not to prepare -- and he did so out of Fear.

Actors consciously or unconsciously take Wrong Actions to deliberately lead them off their career path. Remember, the further they remove themselves from their path, the less they have to face their Fear of Failure or Fear of Success. They feel more comfortable, less at risk, more in control, and it's less work that they have to put toward their career.

It's "Cause and Effect." Actors are fearful of the ramifications of pursuing an acting career (Cause) and thus they take Wrong Actions to avoid it (Effect). More specifically, an actor is afraid that they're not good enough to be an actor (Cause) so they take the Wrong Actions and show up late for class, put off their acting work, sabotage themselves in the audition room, and so on (Effect).

This often starts a chain reaction -- one Wrong Action can lead to another Wrong Action. The actor is not prepared for class one week, and then shows up late the next, and then just doesn't come at all the following week.

Sometimes these Wrong Actions can be influenced by several other factors, including Distractions and Addictions. If you think about it, your Distractions or Addictions can cause you to procrastinate, avoid opportunities, show up late, be unprepared... take Wrong Actions.

Here's a chart to demonstrate what I mean:

Whether the Wrong Actions are influenced directly by your Fear or through the other two Steps to Failure, they all come down to your personal choice. You must learn to recognize Wrong Actions and how dangerous they can be, and then avoid them at all costs. You have to *choose* not to take Wrong Actions. You have to choose to take the Right Actions -- and by choosing Right Actions, it will empower you as an actor.

For the rest of this chapter, I'm going to lay out the most common Wrong Actions I've seen (or see) actors take, be it in their career work, acting class, agent relationships, auditions, meetings, etc. These Wrong Actions are what acting coaches, agents, managers or casting directors might refer to as their "pet peeves." These are by no means all the Wrong Actions an actor can take (nor are they in any particular order), but they are the most prominent.

I'll also share with you the Right Actions that you can take. An actor needs to monitor and train themselves to always take these Right Actions.

With that said, here are The Top 10 Wrong Actions that actors need to avoid (in no particular order), followed by the Right Actions that actors need to embrace.

THE TOP 10 WRONG ACTIONS

- GIVING IN TO FEAR
- EXUDING NEGATIVITY
- BEING UNINFORMED
- BEING UNPREPARED
- PROCRASTINATION
- HAVING POOR RELATIONSHIPS
- TARDINESS
- MISCOMMUNICATION
- DISPLAYING BAD BEHAVIOR
- INACTION

GIVING IN TO FEAR

While Fear is often below the surface, impacting your choices and decisions, it can also creep from your subconscious into your conscious minds as well.

In acting class, you fear what your coach or classmates will think of you and your work. When you land an agent, you fear you will be dropped if you don't immediately book an acting job. In the casting room, you fear that you will "choke" in your audition and the casting director won't ever call you in again.

Giving in to Fear is a Wrong Action. The more you allow yourself to be fearful, the more that Fear will eat away at your desire to be an actor. You will find yourself constantly anxious and nervous, questioning your abilities, and succumbing to that Fear will lead you to neglect your career. Even worse, it could make you needy and desperate for attention, affirmation and support. If you constantly carry this Fear around with you, it will hurt your reputation, your performance and ultimately, your career.

You cannot be fearful of opportunities. You cannot be intimidated by people in positions of power. You cannot fear an acting coach and the work they assign you -- that work is there to help you grow as an actor. You cannot fear your agent or manager and their expectations of you -- they are working to help you succeed.

You cannot fear the casting director. You have to embrace the fact that the casting director *wants* you to do well at the audition (it makes their job that much easier). I know it's easy to think that casting directors have the power to make or break your career, but don't allow yourself to look at them that way. You can't give anyone, even a casting director, that kind of power. It's only one audition... and you'll have many more. There is never "one last chance" for you in this business. You will always create more chances by taking Right Actions. You can't be fearful of the audition process because there are so many factors that are beyond your control.

If you don't get the part, it doesn't mean you did something wrong in the audition or that you're a bad actor. It could be you're just not right for the role, either because you're too tall, too short, too skinny, you have the wrong hair or eye color, you're too good-looking, they found someone with more experience, or they decided to use the producer's neighbor instead. All you can do is prepare, give the audition your all, and be ready to move on if you don't get the part.

Even if you worked hard to prepare but felt like you *didn't* give the best audition (either because you flubbed a line or lost your place in the text), don't worry about it. I can't tell you how many times actors flub something in the audition only to get a callback. What's funny is that sometimes that unintentional flub (and I stress *unintentional*) will relax the actor, alleviating some of their nerves. Suddenly, they become more focused. The pressure's off and they give a stronger audition. Don't be afraid of making a mistake. Casting directors are human too.

You need to relax, release that Fear, go into that auditioned prepared, act professional, and realize that if you don't get this one, there will always be another one. You want to push yourself to do the best you can, whether it's class, meetings or auditions. Don't overburden yourself with unnecessary pressure and Fear.

The Right Actions

- *Acknowledge, experience and work through your Fear.*
- *Talk about your Fears and pressures to family, friends, other actors or even a therapist.*
- *Treat each acting career-related activity with importance without putting unnecessary expectations and pressure on them.*
- *Accept that your acting coach, representation and casting director are there to help you -- they want you to win!*
- *Take pride in your individual efforts. You can't please everyone, so please yourself.*
- *Avoid being desperate and needy. Work on building up your own Confidence rather than needing others to do it for you.*
- *Try your best at each opportunity and then accept that there will be other opportunities. Know that acting is a process and that with time, energy and skill, you will be successful.*
- *No matter the activity, relax and have fun.*

EXUDING NEGATIVITY

Nobody in this business has time for negativity, yet we experience it with actors all the time.

Every acting class has that guy or girl who walks into the room with a cloud of doom hanging over their head. They seem to be cynical, angry, glum, defeated or just plain grim. They often sit in the corner and sulk or brood, unintentionally or intentionally sapping the energy from the room. This negativity is often caused by negative feelings from an event in their life (past or present) that hasn't been resolved, and it permeates everything they do.

It's even worse when actors choose to share their negativity with their coach and class. This negativity can show itself anytime during a class, even in the middle of their scene work. When an actor grumbles, "I'm tired" or "I'm having a bad day," it always brings an uncomfortable hush over the classroom. When they vent about their life or their troubles, that negativity becomes "baggage."

It's okay to experience feelings of anger, sadness or frustration and even bring those feelings to your acting work, if the scene calls for it. When this drama -- this baggage that you carry -- becomes disruptive to your work as well as the work of others, though, then it's a Wrong Action.

It's even *more* detrimental when you bring this baggage to your agent or manager. Your agent or manager probably represents a number of actors and they don't have time to deal with your negativity. Even if they only represent a few actors, time spent dealing with your angry or defeatist attitude is time better spent finding you work. The more negative you are, the less they will want to work *with* you or work *for* you.

This is downright *disastrous* when it comes to auditioning! Bringing your negative energy into an audition will suck the positive energy out of the casting room, leaving the casting director drained and uninterested in you.

When I was a casting director, I had an actor come in for a producer's callback. When I greeted the actor with, "How's it going?" he launched into a diatribe on how his girlfriend was mad at him, he was getting kicked out of his apartment, and his grandfather was going in for hip-replacement surgery.

Neither I, nor the three producers in the room, knew how to respond. He was great for the part and had the right look, but his negativity was off-putting and made us feel uncomfortable. Even though we all felt bad about his situation, we felt nervous about casting him because as one producer said, "This guy's got a lot of drama."

When your coach, agent or casting director asks you, "How's it going?" before class, a meeting or an audition, it's a rhetorical question. You're response should be only positive. It is not an opportunity to vent, complain or garner sympathy. They don't want to hear about your bad day, how you're feeling sick, your empty bank account, or that you have to deal with your father asking you when you're going to get a real job.

There are also those actors who have what I call the "Defeated Actor Syndrome." These are actors that only believe that they are going to fail, that they are doomed to never succeed. They bring their negativity wherever they go: class, an agent meeting and worst of all, the audition. When it comes to the audition, this Defeated Actor Syndrome can present itself at two separate times: **entering the audition** and **exiting the audition**.

When the Defeated Actor enters the audition, before they even open their mouth, they're sending the wrong message to the casting directors. Their body language and attitude is saying "I'm not good enough" and "There's no way I'm going to get this job."

It also happens with actors immediately *after* they finish their auditions. Before the casting director can even decide whether or not to call the actor back, the actor assumes the worst and judges their performance. They might even verbalize their defeatist attitude by saying to the casting director, "I'm sorry, that wasn't very good." They'll exit the room feeling unhappy, rejected, upset and crushed.

The casting director will pick up on this defeatist attitude and this will affect their overall impression of the actor and their performance.

Casting directors do not have the time or patience for negativity. They want to see a prepared, energetic, positive actor who's ready to work and who would be easy to work with on set.

You have to remember that this is a business, and as such, bringing in your negativity is inappropriate. You need to think of each class, meeting and audition as a career opportunity and treat it as such.

The Right Actions

- *Identify your negativity and where it originates. Talk about your issues with family, friends or even a therapist.*

- *Leave your drama at home and your baggage at the door. If you need to take a few minutes to ready yourself, do so. Take a deep breath and exhale the negativity before walking into a class, agent's office or casting room.*

- *Learn to change your negative thoughts into positive thoughts. Review your Affirmations from the Confidence chapter.*

- *Always bring a positive attitude into the room. Be energetic and upbeat.*

- *Keep optimistic about your audition -- before, during and after -- no matter what happens.*

- *When meeting an agent or casting directors, always have a short, positive response ready for when they ask you, "How's it going?"*

- *Be focused, interested and...interesting. Most of all, make your acting work enjoyable!*

BEING UNINFORMED

Knowledge is a vital key to success, and without knowledge, you will be an uninformed actor.

As you've learned, there is a lot more to acting than the acting itself. When it comes to the business side of acting, there are certain rules, tools and processes you need to know in order to be successful. Unfortunately, many actors are simply willfully ignorant to this information, even though it's readily available to any actor that keeps their eyes and ears open.

There's a little more leeway for you new actors that are just moving to Los Angeles and getting acclimated. This mainly applies to those actors who have settled in, but aren't taking classes, don't have headshots, aren't familiar with the top shows or casting directors; those actors that don't know anything about the audition process, what "breakdown," "slate," or "on avail" means. Their unwillingness to learn is a Wrong Action.

Working at an acting career is like any other profession. You have to know what you're walking into. You need to be educated and knowledgeable about your industry. You have to be informed.

There are plenty of resources today, especially with the Internet to help you gather information for your career. You can research acting studios online, "Google" specific agents and managers and use the Internet Movie Database (IMDB.com) to get info on casting directors, directors and your favorite shows. You can even browse industry-related websites to find out what's "hot" in television, what films are being produced and who's casting what.

Beyond that, there is a plethora of actors who are more than willing to share their experience. There are acting coaches, mentors, seminars, classes, books, the industry trades, you name it. Plus, there's always film and television, which is part of your research anyway. Be sure to pay attention to the closing credits.

Being informed starts by getting familiar with the city (so you know where your classes, auditions and studios will be) and studying the craft of acting. It continues with keeping yourself up-to-date about the business and your career. Learning about the business is equally as important as learning about your craft.

The Right Actions

- *Educate yourself. You need to talk to people with experience in the acting business, people you trust for good advice. Take advantage of your CAG and share research and information.*
- *Take classes on both the craft and the business.*
- *Use the Internet. Subscribe to the top acting sites and check them every single day.*
- *Research who's casting the top shows and feature films.*
- *Read as many acting career books as possible, including Judy Kerr's "Acting is Everything."*
- *Subscribe to the industry trade magazines.*
- *Attend seminars and networking events.*
- *Look into joining L.A.-based actor groups such as The Actor's Network and Actorsite.*

BEING UNPREPARED

When it comes to your acting craft, there is no excuse for being unprepared.

I coached an actor (Phil) who was excelling at his craft and appeared ready to get representation and auditions. I set up an appointment for him to meet with a reputable manager. Needless to say, Phil was very excited. The manager e-mailed him two different scenes and gave him a week to prepare.

The day of his manager meeting, I got a call from Phil saying he wanted to schedule a last-minute private coaching session to work on the scenes. I thought it was a smart move to have me help him tweak and refine his audition. But when he showed up for his appointment with me, it was apparent that his scene would need a lot more than tweaking and refining -- Phil hadn't worked on the material *at all*!

He wasn't off book, he knew very little about the script, and he had no "character" -- and his manager meeting was in two hours! Whether it was his naivete or his Fear, Phil honestly thought that he could "wing it," that his acting instincts alone would pull him through. Having little to work with, I coached him as best as I could and sent him on his way.

The manager called me and said he was very disappointed after meeting Phil. He felt that although Phil had a great look and a wonderful personality, he didn't have a grasp of the material and he wasn't ready for representation. The manager passed. I talked to Phil about his lack of preparation. He apologized and said that he learned his lesson: winging it wasn't the way to go. It never is.

You have to be prepared when it comes to the work. Nobody, and I mean nobody, is good enough to wing it when it comes to acting.

As an acting coach, I will often give my students material to take home, scripts to work on either alone or with a partner. After weeks of lectures on the importance of preparation and working on their material outside of class, I trust that they will do the work. Inevitably, there are always students who, when it comes time to perform, are unprepared -- and they always have a poor excuse.

As an agent, I hated getting the call from a casting director that an actor I represented wasn't prepared for an audition. This is the gravest of acting sins. Not only does this Wrong Action affect the actor, it can also hurt your agent's reputation, which will, in turn, hurt your relationship with your agent. I don't care if you only have a couple of hours between hearing about the audition and the actual call time, you need to use that time to *prepare.*

Being unprepared for an audition is also the number one pet peeve for casting directors.

Even though actors are almost always given sufficient time to prepare, casting directors will still see actors bury their nose in their script, searching for their lines on the page. Unprepared actors won't have any character work done or even a sense of the material. They won't know what the show is about or how their character plays into it. They don't even know the genre. They haven't read the stage directions so they don't know whether to sit or stand. They aren't prepared to take adjustments.

Being unprepared makes for bad acting. It is a Wrong Action that will frustrate your acting coach, upset your agent or manager and keep the casting director from hiring you.

The Right Actions

- *Prepare, prepare, prepare.*

- *When it comes to acting class, do your homework. Set aside a specific time each day to work on your material and work on it until it feels ready.*

- *When preparing for your audition, read all the material given to you, including the character breakdown, any extra scenes, any extra lines on the page (even if they're crossed out). If the entire script is available, read it.*

- *Look for information, clues and hints in your audition sides to help you get a better understanding of the story and the characters. WOFAIM and Private Eye your script.*

- *If there is something you don't understand about the script, ask your representation or acting coach before going on your audition.*

- *Read the Audition Tips in the Perseverance chapter.*

- *Enlist the help of a private acting coach if you need guidance tackling a role or preparing for an audition. A coach can help you focus on the nuances of the character and text that could give you a dynamic read.*

PROCRASTINATION

Actors are notorious for the amount of time, effort and energy they put into making up excuses for putting off their work. They will have elaborate tales of danger, disease, disasters, acts of divine power and cosmic circumstances beyond their control.

The truth is…they procrastinated.

Procrastination occurs when you lose sight of the immediate task in front of you, either because the task itself is too overwhelming, you have other priorities you feel you need to focus on, or there is simply something else you'd rather be doing.

Don't get me wrong. I get it. Procrastination is a Wrong Action we all share. It's so easy to look at some daunting work and say, "I'll just do it tomorrow. I'm going to watch TV." Then you keep procrastinating until the very last possible moment. What's the big deal if you still get it done, right?

Well, it is a big deal when it comes to your acting career, especially your career work. There are many talented actors who have lived in Los Angeles for several years that still haven't gotten headshots, done an agent mailing, auditioned for any kind of project, or even taken a class. They come out with plans and dreams to be a successful actor, but they keep finding ways to procrastinate from doing the work.

It's easy to procrastinate, especially in beautiful, sunny L.A., where things are much more laid-back. Monday easily merges into Tuesday, which merges into Thursday, and suddenly it's the weekend and you wonder where the week has gone. If you're not careful, those days merge into weeks, then into months and then suddenly it's three years later and you wonder, "What the hell have I done with my career?"

There is a quote that I like to share with my students:

"Procrastination is the grave in which opportunity gets buried."

If you procrastinate or don't do the work, fewer opportunities will come your way. The more you procrastinate from doing your work, the more you will sacrifice potential opportunities -- the deeper you bury your chance to make it in Hollywood.

It's easy to put off joining an acting class, doing an agent mailing, getting the new headshots your manager asked for, etc. The longer you wait, though, the longer it will take to succeed.

I can always tell the procrastinators in my class. Remember, acting class is a microcosm of your career. I find that what actors put into their craft, they tend to put into their career. If they procrastinate with their class work, chances are they're procrastinating at their career work.

This is wasted potential. They don't take advantage of the financial, physical and emotional investment they've made in an acting class, and both their craft and career suffer.

You need to fight through procrastination and stop that habit before the habit stops you from achieving success.

The Right Actions

- *Read the Perseverance chapter and do the career work outlined. Get into class, put together your Pitch Package, do your research and get to working at your career...now!*

- *Schedule designated times each day for your career work to keep you disciplined and accountable. Set yourself a timeline for getting work done and stick to it.*

- *Make a list of daily, weekly and monthly goals and place it by your computer. Share your goal sheet with your CAG.*

- *Avoid Distractions. If an acting career is a priority, then treat it as such.*

- *When feeling the urge to procrastinate, ask yourself what the possible ramifications of that Wrong Action would be.*

HAVING POOR RELATIONSHIPS

Having a poor relationship with your agent or manager is the fastest way to get dropped.

For some actors, it's a challenge trying to understand their relationship with their representation. Actors will spend quite a bit of time with their agent or manager as they continue on their career path. Sometimes the lines blur as far as what you should expect of each other, how to conduct yourself and what kind of relationship is appropriate.

First and foremost, you have to remember that this is a *business* relationship and you must always treat it as such. Sure, as time goes on you might form a personal relationship with your agent or manager, but it should always start and develop as a business relationship. It will be up to you to understand and be respectful of the boundaries of that relationship.

There are some basic Wrong Actions you can take when it comes to your relationship with your representation.

Poor relationships often start with poor communication. You need to talk with your agent or manager to make sure that you are both on the same page when it comes to your career. It is important for you to discuss with your representation your "type," how they can market you, and a plan or strategy for building your career together as a team.

Your agent or manager is there to help you succeed in your career. They can't do that if they don't know anything about you and your dreams. Having a good relationship with your agent or manager means knowing what to expect of each other, *talking* about your goals, and *listening* to their advice.

That advice can be anything from what to wear to an audition to what photographers to use for headshots to overall career strategy. You need to have your own personal plan, but also be open to your representation's ideas, counsel, experience and vision for you. If you don't trust their judgment or their opinions, then they really can't do anything for you.

On the other hand, you can't rely on your agent or manager for *everything*. You are one of many actors they represent and they can't be at your beck and call. Many agents and managers complain that their clients expect them to drop everything when they call or have a question. True, your representation is there to help, but you need to prioritize when calling them. Don't call to "check in" unless they specifically ask you to do so or you have a specific question that you can't answer yourself. Don't pester your agent or manager...they're too busy getting you work.

Many actors don't know how to appropriately communicate with their representation, especially if they're not getting sent out on auditions. Some whine to their agent or manager and others are more abrasive and demanding -- both are inappropriate.

Whining is not fun to listen to. When someone whines, it's really a passive-aggressive approach to getting something. People whine because they are not getting their needs met and they don't know how to directly ask for what they want. There is nothing worse than an actor coming in to an agent or manager's office, sitting down and whining, "*Whhhhyyyy* am I not getting sent out?"

Equally exhausting and annoying is the aggressive actor who comes in, sits down and demands, "Why am I not getting sent out?!" Being a whiney or demanding actor will get you nowhere. It will only make your agent or manager feel cornered, defensive and irritated...and it may just get you dropped.

Assuming you do have a good working relationship with your representation, you need to be careful that you keep it a *professional* relationship.

I've seen many actors get *too close* to their agent or manager... and that's not always healthy for the actor or the representation. Sure it's fine to go out for coffee, drinks, industry functions or the occasional party. It's even okay to form a friendship with your agent or manager. But when the *personal* relationship interferes with the *business* relationship, things can get messy. You have to remember that it takes a strong, respectful bond to balance both.

The Right Actions

• *Respect your agent or manager. Respect their time and the opportunity you have to work with them.*

• *Build a strong, friendly, healthy business relationship with your representation.*

• *Work with your representation in developing your career.*

• *Listen to and take your representation's advice.*

• *Keep your agent or manager current with what you're doing for your career. Send them the occasional e-mail informing them of career developments; like you're in a new class, working on a student film, or when a casting director gives you a card at an industry function.*

• *If you do need to chat with your representation, set up an appointment to discuss your career -- no random phone calls.*

• *If you're not getting sent out on auditions, instead of whining or pulling attitude with your agent, be positive and proactive. Ask them, "What can I do to help?"*

TARDINESS

Here is a great mantra I discovered that you should always adhere to when going to class, industry meetings, auditions or on the set:

Early is on time.
On time is late.
Late is unacceptable.

As easy-going as Southern California is, the showbiz industry isn't. It is fast-paced and there is always a lot happening. Simply put: coaches, agents, managers, casting directors, producers... nobody has the time to wait for you. And they definitely don't have the patience for your excuses.

Tardiness is perhaps the rudest of the Wrong Actions and it can really rub people the wrong way. Nobody appreciates anyone who's *late*. Being late is disrespectful, plain and simple. Worse yet, it gives you a reputation as someone who can't be relied on. Unfortunately, many actors fall into this habit.

This tardiness trend often begins in class. I had a student who was almost always late to my class. I had a long talk with him and told him that I felt he was being disrespectful. He apologized, but sure enough the following week, he once again walked into class... late. It was disruptive to me as well as the other students. After a while, I had to dismiss him from class. I knew that I had lost an actor with potential, but I hoped it would serve as a wake-up call.

Some of you may think I was a little harsh on him, but sometimes there are lessons that can only be taught through tough love -- this was one of them. Tardiness can come back to haunt an actor in so many ways. Continually coming to class late will eventually get you kicked out. Not calling with a good excuse or not showing up at all will get you kicked out even more quickly.

If you do have to come into class late, be respectful and try to be as quiet as possible. It is very annoying when the student who enters class late makes a big deal out of it for all to see. They scurry into the room, drop their bags with a thud, plop into the chair, put their key chain with 100 keys into their bag, and apologize with an exasperated sigh, "I'm sorry, I'm sorry."

I've often wondered why some actors are always late. Is it their sense of entitlement, that they think they can show up whenever they want? Is it that they don't want to get to class too early because they're uncomfortable talking to the other students? Is it a power trip, thinking they're better than the class? Or is it because they don't have a structured workday and don't know how to manage their time properly? Whatever it is, tardiness produces negative attention.

If tardiness turns into not showing up at all, then you might as well write your own ticket out of this business. Don't be a "no-show, no-call" actor. An acting coach might allow you to miss a class here or there -- as long as there is a good reason -- but if you miss consistently, they'll have no choice but to ask you to leave. They'd rather open up a spot for someone who will be dedicated to learning and growing in their craft.

Tardiness applies to your meetings with your agent or manager as well. They are very busy and often work by a very tight schedule. If you're 15 minutes late, it not only throws off your appointment, but their entire day.

This Wrong Action is even more destructive when it comes to your auditions. Being tardy will strain your relationship with your representation and hurt future casting opportunities.

You should never be late for an audition. You need to show up at auditions early enough to give yourself time to prepare. You need to make sure that you're ready when the casting director calls your name. If you get there at the last second, you won't have time to prep. If they call your name and you're not there, they'll simply move on to the next actor -- and then you've missed an opportunity. So if you have an audition at 2 p.m., show up no later than 1:45 p.m.

If for any reason you are running late to an audition (or you have to miss it), call your representation *immediately.* Be as succinct as possible and let them know when the casting director can expect you ("I'm sorry. The freeway is backed up, please let them know I'll be 10 minutes late"). They'll understand if you're late once or twice -- after all, traffic can be difficult in L.A. Once tardiness becomes habitual, however, then you have a problem.

Being late or not showing up at all is not only inconsiderate and disrespectful, it's also a great way to quickly sabotage your career. When you are purposefully late to a class, meeting or audition, you are blocking yourself from going forward in your acting career. Don't become "that guy" or "that girl."

The Right Actions

- *Remember that "Early is on time," so...*
- *BE ON TIME!*
- *Ask yourself why you're always running late and how it could affect your future opportunities?*
- *BE ON TIME!*
- *Manage your time, plan out your day and be organized -- that will help you avoid being late.*
- *BE ON TIME!*
- *Leave earlier...remember that traffic in L.A. can be a nightmare. Plan your route in advance and even plan an alternate route.*
- *BE ON TIME!*
- *Be respectful of other people's time.*
- *BE ON TIME!*
- *If you find that you are going to be late, make sure to call. Have a good reason why and apologize quickly and sincerely. Assure them it won't happen again.*
- *BE ON TIME!*
- *Attach a Post It on your dashboard that reads: Early is on time. On time is late. Late is unacceptable.*
- *BE ON TIME!*

MISCOMMUNICATION

This Wrong Action specifically addresses phone etiquette. It is about how you conduct yourself on the phone and how to keep any calls with your representation clear, focused, brief and to the point.

First...you need to *answer* your phone.

Chances are, when your representation is calling, it's about an audition, which means there's an urgency to their phone call. It's frustrating to your agent or manager if they can't reach you. Whether it's because your phone is turned off, lost or broken, or you have it set up to block private calls, it's irritating. If getting in touch with you is too much of a hassle, they'll stop trying.

Also, PLEASE have an appropriate (and brief) voice mail message on your phone. There is nothing more annoying than reaching an actor's voice mail only to get sound effects, a jingle, "witty" repartee, a goofy voice, a monologue or a two-minute rap interlude. It might be funny once, but certainly not the third or fourth time.

When your agent or manager does get a hold of you, make sure you always have a pen and paper available to write down the information they're giving to you...and don't lose it! If they reach you while you're driving, you can simply say, "I'll pull over as soon as I can and call you back." Then pull over as soon as you can and call them back!

If you initiate a call to your representation, make sure that you are organized, prepared and clear about what you want. If you need to, write down exactly what you want to say. Also, be articulate: don't stutter, hem and haw, take pregnant pauses or skirt around the topic. Do not waste their time with unnecessary stories, questions or chitchat. Be brief, upbeat and get to the point.

Miscommunication applies to e-mails as well. Agents and managers are using e-mail more frequently to relay information to their clients, especially when it comes to auditions. When your representation does e-mail you, respond back quickly (you should be checking your e-mail several times a day). A simple "Got it, I'll be there, thanks" will do. Also, don't ever send attachments unless your representation requests them as they can clog up their e-mail.

The Right Actions

- *Keep conversations brief and focused.*
- *Know what you want to talk about.*
- *Speak clearly and be pleasant and personable.*
- *Make sure you have a cell phone and headset you can wear so you can take calls and stay mobile.*
- *Check your voice mail often.*
- *Give your agent or manager an alternate phone number. Have an e-mail address as well.*
- *Respond to phone calls and e-mails immediately. Make sure you call from a clear line.*

DISPLAYING BAD BEHAVIOR

When it comes to behavior, there are several Wrong Actions you can take "in the room."

In class, there are actors who can't stop talking. They are constantly whispering to their fellow actors as the teacher lectures, or worse, as a scene is being performed. This "side-talking" is disrespectful and pulls focus in a negative way. Don't make your coach "sshhh" you in class.

Another Wrong Action is not paying attention in the class room by reading magazines, texting, or playing video games on

238 Scott Sedita's Guide To Making It In Hollywood

your phone. By taking these actions, you're disrespecting others in the class as well as yourself.

Then there are those students who can't take direction from their acting coach. Sure, you should be able to talk with your acting coach. I am definitely up for a good discussion about a scene or a role, but you shouldn't argue every note or direction your coach gives you. This forms an untrusting, combative relationship with your acting coach, makes the class feel uncomfortable, and stops you from growing in your craft. If you have a problem with how a coach directs you, have a private conversation with them *after class*. Once again, what you do in the classroom is a microcosm of what you do in the industry.

You also can't carry this bad behavior into your agent or manager meetings. I've heard stories about actors answering their cell phones in the middle of a meeting, being negative and argumentative with their representation, trying to get too personal and even disrespecting their space by putting their feet up on their desk.

If there is ever a place where you need to be on your best behavior, though, it's in the casting director's office. You'd be surprised how many actors not only show up late or unprepared, but also act unprofessionally in the room.

They'll try too hard to impress the casting director by talking about their current project, the showcase they're in, or the last job they booked. Unless the casting director asks you specifically about what you've been doing in your career, this is unwanted information. They'll see it as an intrusion on their time. They often have a lot of actors to audition and they want to keep on schedule. They also have no time for false compliments or flattery. The point is, don't talk too much -- there's a greater chance you'll put your foot in your mouth and talk yourself out of the audition.

You must also act professional in the audition itself. Some actors will ask casting directors unnecessary questions about the script or the character. They'll take a long minute instead of a few seconds to "prepare." They'll choose to paraphrase the text.

They'll question the casting director's adjustment. And the biggest no-no of all, they'll invade the casting director's space when acting -- either by using things in the room as props, pounding on their desk or even going as far as engaging in physical contact with the casting director.

As I mentioned earlier, actors will also have that defeatist attitude. They'll complain about their day, apologize for their audition, sigh, groan and walk out of the casting room crushed. Any casting director will tell you that having anything but a positive, pleasant attitude is the wrong one.

There are also some smaller Wrong Actions which are really more about common courtesy. Don't wear perfume as some people are allergic. Don't come in smelling of cigarettes or alcohol. Also, as some people are more sensitive to germs, don't offer your hand for a handshake -- let them extend the courtesy first, if at all.

Most importantly, don't be a "Diva" or a "Dick."

Throughout my career, I have seen actors who get a taste of success and suddenly turn into Divas and Dicks. They veil their insecurity with a sense of superiority and entitlement that carries into their behavior and work. They don't value anyone else's time or effort and they think the world revolves around *them*. If it's not caught early, that attitude can develop in class, meetings and auditions and blossom fully on the set. If it does, trust me, nobody will want to work with you.

Finally, when attending an industry function, make sure you limit your alcohol intake. Better yet, don't drink at all. You need to be focused, alert and articulate for any conversations you might have as they could lead to career opportunities. You really don't want to be known as that guy or gal who tried to "pick up" a casting director, spilled a drink on the agent, or knocked over a tray of hors d'oeuvres.

The Right Actions

- *In any room, always be respectful of people's time and energy. Spend more time listening rather than talking.*
- *Respect their space.*
- *Take the note or adjustment from the acting coach or casting director.*
- *Stick to the work at hand; stay focused on the material.*
- *Once again, go back and read the Audition Tips in the Perseverance chapter.*
- *Be helpful, ready to work and eager to participate.*
- *Stay positive and charming, and people will remember you.*

INACTION

The best way to fail is to not try.

Therefore, the biggest Wrong Action would be *avoiding* the steps you need to take to be a successful actor...*neglecting* your Talent, Confidence and Perseverance.

As you've read in Section One, you know how important it is to have these Three Steps to Success working in harmony to build an acting career. They go hand in hand, and if you ignore any of them, the others suffer and so does your career.

If you don't work on your Talent -- if you don't study, take classes or ACT -- then you're letting your gift wither and die. Many actors let their craft (their Talent) fade with inaction. You can't deprive your Talent of the work and fine-tuning it needs to survive and thrive. You cannot be an actor without acting.

You also can't be an actor if you don't believe in yourself. It's up to YOU to build Confidence in yourself and in your Talent. Don't let your self doubt and Fear overtake you and control your career moves. More importantly, don't avoid chances to raise your Confidence, whether it's working your craft, implementing your Affirmations, auditioning for roles, and working at your career as much as you can.

Finally, don't be afraid of doing the work. Don't be afraid to learn, to study and mostly…to do the grunt work! You need to have a "Will-Do" attitude. You can have all the Talent and Confidence in the world, but if you don't have Perseverance, you won't have a career.

The Right Actions

- *Take action. Be proactive. Don't let those "three years" pass you by.*
- *Know what you Want: To be a successful actor.*
- *Always work your Talent.*
- *Consistently build your Confidence.*
- *Persevere, persevere, persevere.*
- *Acknowledge your Obstacles.*
- *Identify, experience and overcome your Fear.*
- *Avoid the pitfalls of Distractions, Addictions and Wrong Actions.*
- *Enjoy the acting process, stay positive, and have fun!*
- *Finally, its time to implement your last Affirmation: "I AM A SUCCESSFUL ACTOR." Write it in your Actor's Journal. Say it out loud. Visualize it. Manifest it. Create it…and it will be true! I AM A SUCCESSFUL ACTOR. I AM A SUCCESSFUL ACTOR. I AM A SUCCESSFUL ACTOR…*

SUCCESS STORIES

There is one more step you need to take to make it in Hollywood.

You need to *believe*.

You need to believe that YOU can become a successful actor.

Trust me, if you follow the Three Steps to Success and avoid the Three Steps to Failure, you have a shot, a good shot, to get what you Want. You can live your dream, you can fulfill your destiny.

Just have faith, stay focused, be determined, and get ready to work harder than you've worked at anything in your life. Take advantage of your opportunities, learn from your mistakes, and create your own luck. Always be grateful for the experience, enjoy the journey, and believe in what you're doing.

Celebrate your decision to pursue this profession, embrace your life as an artist, be proud of it, and give it the drive, dedication and work ethic that it deserves...that you deserve.

I want to end this book the same way I end my seminars on making it in Hollywood: with success stories of some actors you most certainly know (although at first, you might not recognize some of their names). There is nothing more inspiring than hearing the stories of other struggling actors who have gone on to achieve great success.

In my years in the industry, I've worked with countless artists who have gone on to wonderful careers. I've chosen these five actors because they embody everything I've discussed throughout this book. They each have Talent, Confidence and Perseverance. While they each took their own path, they refused to let anything stand in their way. Most importantly, they all had a Want to be a successful actor. I hope you learn from their stories and from this book as a whole.

Mostly, I hope you are now even more excited to continue your career as an actor in Hollywood.

WOW, THAT'S WHAT IT TAKES TO BE AN ACTOR

When I was a freshman in the acting program at Boston University, I lived across the hall from a short, stocky, funny kid who was amazingly talented. We became fast friends…as well as an "Odd Couple" of sorts. He was the slightly disheveled, wise-cracking Oscar to my high-strung, anal-retentive Felix. His name was Jay Greenspan.

Truth be told, he was not the best-looking guy in acting school, but he was charming and talented…and incredibly self-confident. To some of us who envied his Confidence, he could seem arrogant. In actuality, at the age of 18, what he had was a great sense of self-worth. He knew who he was and what he wanted, and he had the Confidence to get it. Jay understood his purpose.

Jay was the first person I met on the first day of college. My mother was helping me move into my room, which was right next to the student lounge. As we were carrying boxes, I heard singing coming from the lounge. I opened the door and there was Jay sitting at the piano with his parents standing behind him. I went over to introduce myself, my mother in tow.

I remember Jay's mother saying, "My Jay is so talented…he writes, he acts, he sings." Although Jay was a bit embarrassed by his mother's adulation, it seemed like it wasn't the first time he had heard this. Of course, my mother instantly retorted with an equal attempt at praise on my behalf. But I immediately saw a difference between my mother's belief in me and the adoration that was coming from Jay's mother. As much as my mother loved me, she had just recently accepted my desire to be an actor. It was clear that Jay's parents had encouraged him and his creative aspirations his whole life.

You could see how that 18 years of belief, faith and support had instilled Confidence in him. He was Confidence personified. He was focused and he had the Talent to back it up. Jay walked around as if he was already a successful actor.

Although Jay's work in acting class was always good and had a natural progression, there was one specific time where his Talent (and his self-Confidence) came into question. Ultimately, it was his belief in himself and his unflinching Perseverance that pushed him through.

One day in acting class, Jay performed a Shakespearean monologue...and it didn't go well. Whether it was an odd choice or that he didn't go deep enough into the work, the professor ripped into him in front of everybody (as only a *college* acting professor could). Jay had never gotten such harsh criticism in class before. You could see the look of disappointment on Jay's face.

Later that afternoon, I walked over to Jay's dorm room to console him. I recommended that the best thing to do when feeling sad or rejected is to have a pity party...just like I would! But Jay had other ideas. He told me to go ahead and have a pity party without him. So...I did!

When I came back a few hours (and a few beers) later, I walked by Jay's room. The door was closed, but I heard him shouting. It was passionate, spirited, full of emotion. As I slowly opened the door, I immediately felt heat emanating from the room. Every light was on. I could smell sweat, as if he had been working out for hours.

I peeked my head in and I saw Jay pacing. He was in the Acting Zone. The look on his face was intense. He was working on his Shakespeare monologue from class that day. He was so immersed in his work that he never saw me standing there. I quietly closed the door and walked across the hall to my dorm room. As I opened my door, I felt a very different vibe. My room was dark, cool and untouched...no work had been done there.

The next day in class, Jay asked the professor if he could perform his monologue again and the professor said no, telling him he needed more time to work on it. Jay persisted and the professor relented. Jay took the stage, paused for a moment, and then did his piece. After he finished, there was silence in the classroom, followed by a round of applause. He nailed it. I mean, he was terrific...even the professor thought so.

It was at that moment, sitting in class, that I thought, "Wow, that's what it takes to be an actor."

I realized how much an actor needs to Want it, how much they have to believe in themselves, and how they need to fight through rejection and disappointment. I realized that you can't sit back and have a pity party. Instead you have to rebound, you have to jump back in. You have to sweat so much that you smell up your room with your passion, your drive and your Talent.

What Jay did in that *class* is what an actor always needs to do in their *career*. You need to take the feedback, no matter how good or bad, go back home, work on improving, and then fight to present it.

Jay always had the Talent and the Confidence, but he showed that he also had the Perseverance. That's a microcosm in time, but that moment defines a career. Jay Greenspan later became known as Jason Alexander.

WHO'S THAT GIRL?

I represented Courteney Cox when I was an agent in New York. She was 19 years old, brand new to the business and had little training...but there was something very special about her. She had a unique look: she was a beautiful Southern tomboy with short-cropped hair, sparkling blue eyes and a Colgate smile. She had a positive disposition and a great self-deprecating sense of humor, which counteracted her new actor insecurities.

I sent Courteney out on auditions and it didn't take long for casting directors to take notice. While she began booking commercials and building her reputation in the business, we never expected what was about to happen next.

It was the early '80s and music videos were emerging as a mainstream form of entertainment, all due to the birth of MTV. As MTV grew in its popularity, music videos became a great opportunity for new actors to get work. Even established directors wanted to be part of this new, exciting medium. Because I handled many young actors, I was busy booking my clients in a number of music videos for top '80s artists.

I got a call from a casting director requesting an actress to appear in a music video. It was for Bruce Springsteen's new single, *Dancing in the Dark*. The casting director wanted a teenage girl with lots of personality, big hair (it was the '80s after all), who could dance. I instantly thought of Courteney. Even though she had very short hair and no "dance training," I knew her infectious personality would get her noticed.

But Courteney didn't want to go on the audition. She didn't think she could dance, especially in front of other people. In fact, she was petrified at the thought. I assured her there was no choreography involved, that she just had to be herself and... *dance!*

After the audition, she came back to my office very upset with me. She said, "Scott, that was the worst audition I have ever been on. I was totally wrong for the part. All the girls there could dance...and they all had big hair!"

I felt horrible. My thinking "outside-the-box" backfired and left my client feeling embarrassed and humiliated. I was a bad agent.

Then the phone rang. It was the casting director calling to say they loved Courteney and wanted to bring her in for a callback. Maybe I was a good agent.

I had to sit Courteney down and convince her to go to the callback. I reassured her that the casting director loved her and that this could be a good career opportunity. It was not only a chance to be seen, but also to work with one of the '80s most prominent directors, Brian DePalma.

Courteney relented and went on the callback. After her meeting, she returned to my office...beaming. She told me that she and DePalma talked for a while and got along great...and then he asked her to dance. Using her self-deprecating sense of humor to diffuse her anxiety, she told him, "Believe me, you really don't want to see me dance...it will ruin your day." DePalma laughed... and Courteney danced.

A few days later, Courteney was on a plane to St. Paul to shoot the video at a live Springsteen concert. You can only imagine how she felt dancing in front of thousands of people!

When the *Dancing in the Dark* video premiered on MTV, it became an overnight sensation for Springsteen as well as the unknown girl from Alabama. When Springsteen sang out "Hey, baby," tossed his mic over his shoulder, and reached for Courteney's hand, she not only jumped on stage to dance with The Boss, she also jumped into the limelight. Her slightly embarrassed, excited "oh-my-God-he-picked-me" reaction won over viewers as well as the industry. The next day, my phone didn't stop ringing. Everybody asked...

"Who's that girl?"

From the moment the video debuted, Courteney got opportunities to audition and she took advantage of all of them. She appeared in many national commercials and guest star roles. She worked as a cover girl on a Noxzema campaign, appeared on Johnny Carson's *The Tonight Show* and eventually booked a series regular role on the short-lived TV show *Misfits of Science*. Her most recognizable role at the time, however, was Alex P. Keaton's girlfriend Lauren on the show *Family Ties*.

Courteney had the Talent and the Confidence, but it was going to be her ability to stay in the game -- her Perseverance -- that was now going to be tested.

As is often the case with overnight sensations, the offers eventually began to slow down. After *Family Ties,* Courteney continued to work, appearing in some films and TV shows. But for the next four or five years, she essentially fell off the Hollywood radar.

Nevertheless, Courteney persevered. With her contagious personality, charm, sense of humor and work ethic, Courteney didn't give up. She kept working and it paid off...again! After a few years, Courteney Cox got her next big break by booking a little show called *Friends*.

YOU, I WANT TO REPRESENT

When I was an agent in New York, I met a young actress I was interested in representing and told her to get a scene together with a partner. She did all the right things an actor should do when performing a scene for an agent. She found a scene that had depth and emotion and one that was driven by her character. She also picked a scene opposite a male character -- agents like to see the male/female dynamic.

The young actress was good, but it was her scene partner who interested me the most. That actor was Christopher Meloni.

Even though his part was minimal, Chris fascinated me. His listening, his reacting, his stillness and his Confidence in himself left a strong impression. This was a well-trained actor. At the end of the scene, I told the actress that I'd be in touch. She thanked me, and as she left, I grabbed Chris and said, "You, I want to represent."

I set up a meeting with Chris and he told me about himself. He said that after graduating from an acting program, he came out to New York, continued to train and tried to get representation...for four years! He was often told by agents that he was talented, but "too old." The sad thing was...Chris was only 26.

I believed in him, so I signed him.

Although he had no professional credits on his resume, Chris had Talent and a belief in his Talent. I found Chris to be very focused. He took all the right actions: going to class, auditioning for student films, doing anything and everything he could to get noticed...even being willing to help a friend perform a scene in front of an agent.

Also, at the time, *Moonlighting* was a hit show and its star Bruce Willis was a hot commodity. To me, Chris was a younger Bruce Willis. He had a wise-cracking, glib sensibility, but he was also intense and showed signs of great vulnerability behind his "guy's guy" exterior. He understood who he was and that gave Chris a great deal of Confidence.

I knew that once I got Chris out there for the right roles, he would book. Because of Chris' age and my reputation of only working with young adults, I had to really work hard to pitch him to casting directors.

I remember talking to Lynn Kressel -- one of New York's leading casting directors at the time -- about bringing Chris in for a show she was working on. I had a good relationship with Lynn, but she was cautious about seeing Chris because of his lack of credits.

I told her that she "either see Chris *now* or try to get him in a year when he's with William Morris and too busy." We both laughed at the reality of that possibility. She brought Chris in to read for a co-star role of a terrorist on a show called *The Equalizer*. He booked it.

Chris was so excited he finally got his "big break" that he invited some people over to his apartment to watch his TV debut. We got to Chris' scene and he was wearing a ski mask. Chris said, "Wait, wait...they're going to pull my ski mask off." Unfortunately, as is often the case, Chris' big reveal got left on the cutting-room floor, and we never saw his face. Not only that, when Chris' character spoke...it wasn't even his voice. For whatever reason, they had dubbed over his lines with another actor.

After four-plus years of waiting for his chance, his big break didn't feature his face or even his voice. Nobody could tell it was Christopher Meloni. Nevertheless, Chris didn't allow what happened to deter him. He still considered his first TV appearance a victory, and he was determined to experience and celebrate many more victories. He knew the best way to do that was to find more work.

His determination paid off and Chris went on to book. He immediately became the Prince of the New York commercial scene. He appeared in several commercials where he could showcase his funny, easy-going persona, his "macho-guy-in-peril" personality.

He booked a series regular in the HBO original show *1st & Ten*, which lead him to star in the short-lived sitcom, *The Fanelli Boys*. Chris went on to do several pilots, made-for-TV movies and feature films including *Bound* and *Runaway Bride*. This eventually lead Chris to great success, starring simultaneously as a series regular on two hit TV shows, HBO's *Oz* and NBC's *Law & Order: SVU*.

Chris told me that his early years of struggle gave him a strong work ethic and an appreciation for what he has now. As an actor, persevering means being willing to struggle every single day and enjoying the struggle, knowing that it will eventually lead you to where you want to be, knowing that eventually you *will* work.

THE PICTURE OF JOSH DUHAMEL

Josh Duhamel came to my acting studio in 1999. He had never studied acting before. He was handsome, charming and affable. I liked him immediately, mainly because he had a great sense of humor about himself.

At our initial meeting, Josh told me that he wasn't sure if he was an actor...or, for that matter, if acting was something he wanted to pursue. He did say, though, that he had a desire to test the waters, to explore the craft. So, I put him in my acting class.

Once I saw Josh's work, I immediately knew he had the Acting Gene -- he had the potential to be a good actor. However, I wasn't sure yet if he had the commitment it takes to have a career.

In my acting class, Josh found a safe place where he could explore his creativity. Like many young actors, at first he struggled with being honest in his work. I would often yell out at him, "I don't believe you!" Josh was not to be deterred. He had the courage and conviction to dig deep inside himself and find the truth in his acting...and the more he found the truth in his acting, the more he embraced being an actor.

As I gave Josh techniques to access his emotions and open up his imagination, he learned how to tap into his Talent. Josh was a sponge and within months, he began to show progress in his work. He started to get more and more excited about not only the prospect of becoming an actor, but also having a career.

Josh got an agent and started to go out on auditions. The more we worked together on his auditions, the more he became committed to the craft.

But it wasn't until he got an audition for an independent film, *The Picture of Dorian Gray*, that I really saw how committed he could be. Josh wanted the role of Dorian Gray and worked intensely to prepare himself for the audition. He carried around the script, talked about the screenplay and the character, and immersed

254 Scott Sedita's Guide To Making It In Hollywood

himself -- mind, body and soul. He *became* Dorian Gray and eventually, Josh got the role.

Josh was invested and committed to doing the best work that he could in that film. That meant fully understanding the text, his character's Want, history, emotional state, inner thoughts, stakes and urgency of the circumstances.

After completing the film, he made an appointment to coach with me on a role for the soap *All My Children*. Since he was filming on location, I hadn't seen Josh in a while. When he walked into my studio, I was looking at a very different Josh Duhamel. He was focused, committed, confident, driven and passionate. He was a professional actor.

After working with him on his audition for *All My Children*, I knew Josh would get the role. He flew out to New York, screen-tested and booked the job. He went on to win the Daytime Emmy for his role as Leo du Pres on *All My Children*.

Three years after his soap contract ended, he was snatched up to star in the feature film *Win a Date with Tad Hamilton!* as well as the TV show *Las Vegas*. Josh Duhamel is a perfect example of somebody who had the Talent, chose to embrace it, and brought an intense commitment to his craft, which lead him to a successful career.

ONE DAY, I'M GOING TO BE THE NEXT MERYL STREEP

It was the winter of 1981. I had already left the acting department at Boston University and was attending Film School across the street.

One of the first things they taught us newbie directors at Film School was that actors were called "talent," which essentially meant movable props. It was recommended that we use non-actors for our initial films because the concentration should be on "getting the shot" (lighting, camera angle, etc...everything that's vital to becoming a filmmaker). Because we were encouraged to use our friends and roommates, we aspiring directors were never taught how to direct, connect or even talk with actors. I hear things have changed...slightly.

I had come from acting school with the purpose of directing actors on film, so the thought of working with non-actors was unacceptable. From the first day I set foot in film school and began shooting my projects, I would only use trained actors. Considering my time spent in the theatre department, I knew lots of them. They were my friends and I knew they were hungry to explore the film side of acting. By my senior year, I was the first film student to lobby for and get actors school credit for appearing in a B.U. film school project.

One of those B.U. actors I cast the most was a young woman by the name of Julie Smith. There was something captivating about Julie. She was down-to-earth but always the optimist. She was focused yet spontaneous. She had a great sense of humor about herself and about life. Julie had red hair, porcelain skin and a vibrant smile. She was plain, yet breathtakingly beautiful. She had Talent...and lots of it.

By the time I graduated, I had directed Julie in five films (albeit student films). She was fun to work with, incredibly hard-working and eager to learn. She was always willing to act, which was perfect for this aspiring filmmaker who would call on a moment's notice when feeling inspired.

One of those "inspired" moments was a morning after a major snowstorm in Boston. I was in the midst of working on a short comedic film about a lovable loser who fantasized about being with his secret love...Julie. In his fantasy, I was going to spoof the lover's "walk-on-the-beach" scene in the film, *The Way We Were.* After the snowstorm hit, I thought instead, I'll spoof the snow scene from *Love Story*...you know, when the star-crossed lovers make snow angels, playfully throw snow balls at each other, roll in the snow, and ultimately end up kissing.

At 8 a.m. on a Sunday morning, I called Julie and the film's leading man and had them meet me at the Common, a well-known public park in Boston. It was a beautiful day. The park was empty. All the storm clouds had past, leaving a clear blue sky above. The grounds of the Common were blanketed white with fresh snow... and it was cold!

As the male actor whined about the freezing temperature and danced around trying to stay warm, Julie stayed calm and collected. She kept herself warm with the excitement and anticipation of the shoot...she was doing what she loved.

After an hour of filming, we took a break. I went over to Julie. In her wool cap, with her red hair draping down over her parka, she looked absolutely gorgeous. I said, "You know Julie, one day, you're going to be a star." She looked up at me and smiled. With a humble self-assurance, Julie said, "One day, I'm going be the next Meryl Streep."

Julie Smith became Julianne Moore. Twenty years later, sitting at home watching the Oscars, I watched Julie walk down the red carpet with Meryl Streep for *The Hours.* I felt a great sense of awe for that young woman who had such faith in herself, knew what her destiny was, and had the Talent, Confidence and Perseverance to make her dreams come true.

INDEX

About the Author

Scott Sedita is one of the most well-respected and busiest acting coaches in Hollywood.

He's starred as the Acting Coach on the E! series *Fight For Fame* and has appeared often on USA Network's *Character Fantasy*, Fox Sports Network's *Helmets Off* and MTV's *Adventures In Hollyhood*. He is also the author of the best-selling comedy book, "The Eight Characters of Comedy, A Guide to Sitcom Acting and Writing," which has propelled Scott to work as a comedy consultant for sitcoms in both the U.S. and Canada.

A graduate of Boston University's Film and Television program, Scott has more than 25 years of experience in the entertainment industry. He began his career in New York as a talent agent, where he helped to launch the careers of many of today's top stars, including Courteney Cox, Matt LeBlanc, Christopher Meloni, Dylan Walsh, Jerry O'Connell, Vincent D'Onofrio and Teri Polo, to name a few.

In 1990, Scott relocated to Los Angeles where he worked as a sitcom writer for Howie Mandel, Bobcat Goldthwait and many others. In the mid-90s, Scott worked as a casting director for Danny Goldman Casting until launching his Scott Sedita Acting Studios in 1998.

Today, Scott and his staff teach the craft of acting to the hundreds of actors who walk through his doors on a weekly basis. Scott has coached and taught some of today's hottest talent, including Josh Duhamel, Jennifer Finnigan, Chace Crawford, Brandon Routh and many others who star in films, soaps, prime time dramas and sitcoms.

Scott continues to teach his guide to making it in Hollywood in motivational seminars across the country.

SCOTT SEDITA

ACTING STUDIOS

where the actor's craft
and career come together

526 N. Larchmont Blvd.
Los Angeles, CA 90004
Phone: 323-465-6152
Fax: 323-465-6202
www.ScottSeditaActing.com
www.myspace.com/ScottSeditaActingStudios

Order Form

Fax Orders: (323) 465-6202
Telephone Orders: (323) 465-6152. Have your credit card ready.
E-mail Orders: **AtidesPub@aol.com**
Postal Orders: Atides Publishing, Scott Sedita, 526 N. Larchmont Blvd., Los Angeles, CA 90004, USA.

Please send me _____ copies of "Making It In Hollywood."

Please send me more FREE information on:
__Classes __Seminars __Mailing Lists __Consultation

Name:_____
Address:_____
City:_____ State:____
ZIP:_____
Telephone:_____
Email address:_____

Sales Tax: Please add 7.75 percent for products shipped to California addresses.

Shipping By Air
U.S.: $4.00 extra for first book and $2.00 for each additional book.
International: $9.00 extra for first book; $5.00 for each additional book.

Payment: __Check   __Credit Card:
__Visa   __Master Card   __American Express

Card Number:_____
Name on card:_____ **Exp. Date**_____